# GAMES GALORE
# FOR
# CHILDREN'S PARTIES
# AND MORE

by Shari Ann Pence

*80 fun games and activities for parties, classrooms,
youth groups, carnivals, company picnics,
rainy days and special occasions*

Illustrated by: Priscilla Burris

**Fun castle** ™
publications

Riverside, California

Second Edition

Library of Congress Catalog Card Number: 95-90818

ISBN 0-9645771-1-9


Content Editor:  Debra Stearns
                 Marriage, Family and Child Counselor
Copy Editor:  Rosemary Kohout
Field Research Assistants:  Pamela Anderson and Sarah Renee Pence

Funcastle Publications
P.O. Box 51217
Riverside, CA 92517
(951) 653-5200
www.partygamesgalore.com

Manufactured in the United States of America

---

---

\*\*\*\*\*\*\*\*\*\*\*\*\*\*\*\*\*\*\*\*\*\*\*\*\*\*\*\*\*\*\*\*\*\*\*\*\*\*\*\*\*\*\*\*\*\*\*\*\*\*\*\*\*\*\*\*\*\*\*\*\*\*\*\*\*

## *Acknowledgements*

\*\*\*\*\*\*\*\*\*\*\*\*\*\*\*\*\*\*\*\*\*\*\*\*\*\*\*\*\*\*\*\*\*\*\*\*\*\*\*\*\*\*\*\*\*\*\*\*\*\*\*\*\*\*\*\*\*\*\*\*\*\*\*\*\*

My heartfelt thanks to the wonderful people who shared their encouragement, support, talent and wisdom in the production of this book:

Sarah and Brandon Pence

My parents, Ron and Marilyn Bacon

My dear friends Pamela Anderson,
Rosemary Kohout and Debra Stearns

\*\*\*\*\*\*\*\*\*\*\*\*\*\*\*\*\*\*\*\*\*\*\*\*\*\*\*\*\*\*\*\*\*\*\*\*\*\*\*\*\*\*\*\*\*\*\*\*\*\*\*\*\*\*\*\*\*\*\*\*\*\*\*\*\*

and special thanks to...

Priscilla Burris

Robin Davis Miller and Kenneth Gabor,
The Authors Guild, Inc.

Paul de Jonckheere of Commercial Electronics

Jan Mecklenburg,
The Society of Children's Book Writers and Illustrators

Karen Sevaly of Teacher's Friend Publications, Inc.

\*\*\*\*\*\*\*\*\*\*\*\*\*\*\*\*\*\*\*\*\*\*\*\*\*\*\*\*\*\*\*\*\*\*\*\*\*\*\*\*\*\*\*\*\*\*\*\*\*\*\*\*\*\*\*\*\*\*\*\*\*\*\*\*\*

A very big *Thank You*
to all of the children who participated in our field research:

Sarah and Brandon Pence♥Heather, Jonathan and Laura Anderson
Tara Deleeuw♥Janelle, Laura and Paul Burris♥Nichole and Danny Maguire
Stacey and Tami Walbring♥Angie Quiroz♥Katie Varchetto♥Danny Nevil

...and the children of The Kids' Place in Beaumont, California

\*\*\*\*\*\*\*\*\*\*\*\*\*\*\*\*\*\*\*\*\*\*\*\*\*\*\*\*\*\*\*\*\*\*\*\*\*\*\*\*\*\*\*\*\*\*\*\*\*\*\*\*\*\*\*\*\*\*\*\*\*\*\*\*\*

# Table of Contents

## Everybody Wins    37

## Tossing Games    49

## Quiet Games    59

## Active Games    71

## Ready-to-Copy Games    *83*

## Noncompetitive Activities    *93*

## Farewell Activities    *107*

## Theme Party Index    *117*

## Index    *118*

## Ready-to-Copy Game Solutions    *120*

# *Introduction*

The most popular form of entertainment for children's birthday parties is games, games and more games. But, if the thought of playing another round of musical chairs, pin-the-tail on the donkey or hot potato makes you want to beg and plead with your child to settle for a party away from home, don't get on your knees just yet. Instead, take a look at these new exciting games for children to enjoy.

Your guests will be pleasantly surprised when you introduce contemporary games that are fun and easy to learn. Each game outlines the following: Age range, game time for eight players, materials needed, preparation, how to play and suggestions for low cost prizes and favors. Also included is a storytelling introduction to lead the children into the explanation of the rules for the game.

Entertaining your guests with the games and activities in this book will enable you to personally experience the joy of celebrating with your child.

# HOW TO BENEFIT THE MOST FROM THIS BOOK

I suggest you take a moment to read the definitions of the following steps for each game and activity. The step-by-step instructions are provided to help you host the games and activities with ease.

## For Ages:

The age considerations were selected based on children's abilities, the safety of game supplies, short or long attention spans and the general interests of particular age groups.

It's best to observe your child's abilities and current stage of development and gear your selections accordingly. Chances are you'll be right on the mark with their friends and classmates, as well.

## Time:

Each game and activity lists the approximate time it takes eight children to participate. This will help you prepare a schedule of games and activities to fill the time needed for entertaining your guests.

Eight is the magic number because it is an ideal group of children to manage for party games and activities. You can play these games with as few or as many guests as you wish, but I don't recommend more than twelve in a party situation.

## Materials Needed:

A complete list of everything you need will help you determine if you can add the game or activity to your party based on the cost and availability of materials needed.

## Preparation (Before the party):

What you need to do before the day of the party to make the craft activities ready to make or the games ready to play.

To make game hosting easier place the supplies, prizes and favors for each game or activity in a large paper grocery bag and label it with the title of the game or activity. During the party you'll have everything you need ready to go and right at your fingertips.

## Preparation (Before you begin):

What you need to do before the children begin the craft activity at the party.

## Preparation (Before you play):

What you need to do before the children start to play the game at the party.

## Introducing the Game:

Setting the scene for the game will delight the children and help them understand the rules on how to play.

## How to Play:

After you captivate your audience with the brief storytelling introduction, explain the rules for how to play the game. If you'd like to demonstrate the game with a practice run it will help the children visualize the object of the game. Their enthusiasm will be greater when they know exactly what needs to be done. When teaching new games and activities, be sure to ask if everyone understands the rules on how to play before you begin.

## Prizes and Favors:

Keep in mind these are only suggestions. Choose what you can easily afford or have available.

Have extra prizes and favors on hand for the following reasons: Some parents who remain at the party with their child may bring a sibling. Prizes or favors may get broken or lost. It's always better to have too many than not enough.

# TIPS FOR GAME PLANNING

## Making a Schedule

The ideal party schedule includes an arrival activity, games, refreshments, gift opening and a farewell activity. If you want your party to last 2 hours plan on a 15 minute arrival activity, 45 minutes of games, refreshments for 30 minutes and the gift opening to take 20 minutes. Close the party with a 10 minute farewell activity and you can easily fill a 2 hour period.

What if things don't go according to my plan? This is true of almost every party I've hosted or attended. When children are involved, there is no such thing as clockwork. It's extremely important to be relaxed and willing to change your schedule to accommodate your guests. The schedule is only an outline to help you manage the party with ease. Flexibility is the key to ensure it's success.

## Selecting Games and Activities

The most important thing to remember when selecting games for a celebration is to include your child. Who knows best which games will be the hit of the party? Make a preliminary list of the games you can do based on availability and cost of materials. Review some of the games with your child and choose their favorites. Surprises are nice, so now that you know the types of games your child will like best, pick 2 or 3 more and add them to the line-up.

If your child is too young to decide, use their personality as a guide. Do they like to help you with the dishes? Play "Dishpan Derby." Maybe they enjoy giving the dog a bath, choose "Give That Dog a Bath." Include them in the game plan by selecting games that involve a few of their favorite things.

## Planning Games for Special Events

Use the party suggestions when planning games for classrooms, youth group meetings and other special occasions. Select games based on the ages of the children who will be in attendance. The time guidelines will give you an idea of how many games to plan for their entertainment.

If you are planning a carnival or company picnic, ask for volunteers to lead groups of children in different games and activities to keep the entertainment moving at a steady pace. There are many exciting games and relays in this book that will make any special event extraordinary.

# TIPS FOR GAME PLANNING

## The Game Plan

Now that you've decided how long the game portion of your party or special event will last, add the times of your selections to be sure you have planned enough games. Add 2 to 4 more games to your game plan in case you need to keep the children entertained for a little longer.

Write down the order in which you'd like to play the games. It's a good idea to follow up a relay or active game with a quiet game or activity. By alternating active and quiet games you can maintain a balance in the children's energy levels and keep the party manageable.

## Rainy Day Plan

No one can predict what Mother Nature will do on the day of your party, so it's always best to have an indoor plan. Most of the games in this book can be played in or out of doors. If you've selected a few games or relays that can only be played outside, choose and prepare a few alternate games for a rainy day plan.

# SAMPLE GAME PLAN #1

Party Theme:  Camping/Slumber Party

For Ages:  8 to 10 years old

Time planned for games:  45 minutes

| | Game Time |
|---|---|
| Arrival Activity: Lunch Sack Favor Keeper | |
| 1.  Early Bird Relay | 3 minutes |
| 2.  Hiking Trail Scavenger Hunt | 15 minutes |
| 3.  Man in the Moon | 10 minutes |
| 4.  Marshmallow Moon Rock Toss | 4 minutes |
| 5.  Funny Ghost Stories | 10 minutes |
| 6.  Smelly Gym Socks | 3 minutes |
| 7.  Creepy Critters | 10 minutes |
| Farewell Activity:  Picture Postcards | |
| TOTAL TIME OF GAMES SELECTED: (not including arrival and farewell activities) | 55 minutes |

*By scheduling 55 minutes of games, you're assured plenty of entertaining activities to fill a 45 minute time period for your guests.

*Pick 2 easy-to-prepare, noncompetitive games (you won't need prizes) as extras:

•In For a Landing        •Monkey Shines

If the children rise and shine a little early the following morning, you'll have additional games ready to entertain them before the farewell activity. Extra games can also be played when the pizza's not delivered on time or if someone forgot to pick up the cake. Any time delays in your party can be filled with games and activities.

NOTE: There is a balance in the lengths and types of activities as well as a good combination of active and quiet games. List your selections and mix the order until you have a well-balanced schedule.

# SAMPLE GAME PLAN #2

Party Theme:  Happy Birthday Animal Lovers

For Ages:  4 year olds

Time planned for games:  30 minutes

|  |  | Game Time |
|---|---|---|
| Arrival Activity:  Patchwork Turtle | | |
| 1. Bowling Alley Cats | | 5 minutes |
| 2. Picnic on an Ant Hill | | 3 minutes |
| 3. Give That Dog a Bath | | 8 minutes |
| 4. Monkey Shines | | 6 minutes |
| 5. Cat and Mouse | | 8 minutes |
| 6. Star Gazing | | 10 minutes |
| Farewell Activity:  Maracas | | |

TOTAL TIME OF GAMES SELECTED:        40 minutes
(not including arrival and farewell activities)

*By scheduling 40 minutes of games, you're assured plenty of entertaining activities to fill a 30 minute time period for your guests.

*Pick 2 easy-to-prepare games as extras:

    •Dishpan Derby         •Storybook Memory Game

Theme parties are fun and can make planning the celebration and games easier, but you shouldn't be concerned if games and activities do not relate to a chosen theme. In the field research "parties" I hosted, the children participated in a variety of games and activities that didn't focus on a main theme. The "parties" were a huge success and by the children's rave reviews I could see the games and activities were related in one very special way, they were lots of fun for everyone! If you would like to include theme related games and activities, see the "Theme Party Index" on page 117 for suggestions.

# TIPS FOR GAME HOSTING

## A Little Help From Your Friends and Relatives

Call upon a friend or relative to assist you at the party to help you with the games and activities, serving refreshments, gift opening and clean up. Assign the duties each of you will be responsible for during the party. Remember to show your appreciation by sending a thank you card, inviting them to lunch or by offering to return the favor at their child's next party.

Teenagers are great party assistants. They gladly accept fun, money-making opportunities. Offer to pay more than a babysitter's regular fee; it will be a good investment. Clearly define what their duties will be throughout the party.

## Siblings

Older siblings will feel special on this day if you allow them to help with the games and activities. They can help you set up the games and assist the younger children with the craft activities. They can retrieve the items tossed in the carnival style games. If a relay calls for an even numbered player, they can fill the space. Assign them the duty of "prize monitor" to hand out the prizes and favors for each game.

Helping with the games is more fun than a chore. They'll be delighted with the responsibility and feel as though they contributed to the success of the party. Be sure to award them a special prize for their assistance.

## Candid Moments

Ask an "aspiring" amateur photographer to take pictures during the games (a friend, neighbor or relative). Children are the best models when they're too busy having fun to notice the camera. You'll have some great candid shots to add to their memory book for the party.

# TIPS FOR GAME HOSTING

## Me First!

Here are some lining-up tips to help you avoid conflicts for the order of play:

Announce that the birthday child will be first in line for all of the games. Everyone knows it's their special day and most of the children will be more than willing to step aside. This will allow you to line up everyone behind the birthday child. If there is a struggle over who will be next in line, you can determine the order by announcing "shortest to tallest," "ladies first," "youngest to oldest" or "A,B,C order." Inform the children this will be the order of play for each game and make a game of it. Tell the children to remember who is in front of them and line up behind that person every time.

If two children are fighting in line, change the order and put a few children in between them so they can't reach one another. It should immediately stop the conflict.

Make an announcement to encourage quick and orderly behavior, such as "the faster we line up, the more games we can play" or you can offer a special treat to be awarded to all at the end of the games if they've been on their best line-up behavior.

## It's My Party and I'll Cry if I Want to

There is always a possibility the guest of honor will be out of sorts with all of the attention and excitement, so it's wise to have both parents in attendance at the party. If that's not possible, designate a special helper such as a babysitter, a willing grandparent or a relative to assist you in this or any other crisis that might take you away from the party.

If your child (or a child without supervision) becomes unruly, have the designated helper quietly lead them away from the party area. While remaining in full view of the fun and games, explain they may join in after they take a moment to calm down. By separating them from the festivities, their behavior should improve when they see the party can and will go on without them.

# TIPS FOR GAME HOSTING

## Sitting on the Sidelines

Some children are inhibited when it comes to playing games. If a child says they do not wish to play, please don't ask several times "are you sure you don't want to play?" Instead, quietly say to them "That's all right, but if you think you'd like to join in later that would be okay, too."

One thing I have found to work with shy children is to let them watch the other guests to see exactly how the game is played. Then if the game allows, I pick it up and take it to where they are seated and ask "would you like to try from here?" Soon they are lining up with the rest of the guests to join in the fun. If they say no, I quickly move on to the next game. Be sure to include them when it comes to handing out favors for each game whether or not they participated.

## Encore, Encore

If a game is a hit and the majority of the children want to play it again, let them. Your schedule of games is designed to be flexible. By allowing the children to play their favorite games more than once you can stretch the game plan. For games 7 minutes or longer, play only twice. For games under 6 minutes, play two or three times. Observe the children's enthusiasm while participating to determine if another round should be played or if it would be best to move on to the next game or activity.

Prizes for encore games can be any of the following: a round of applause or a standing ovation (all encores deserve a standing ovation!), fruit snacks, stickers, hand stamp or a consolation prize not needed for another game. Be sure to announce the prize before beginning the next round so the children won't expect the same prize to be awarded.

## Have Fun

Children enjoy watching a grown-up laugh, play and act just plain silly. You don't have to make an absolute fool of yourself, but do please have some fun! If you've ever wanted to go back to your childhood, this is a great opportunity to do so and share it with your child.

# TIPS FOR GAME HOSTING

## Tips for Toddlers

Some of the games in this book can include toddlers in the event younger siblings, relatives or friends attend the party. Structured games and activities aren't really recommended for an entire group of two or three year old's because of their temperaments.

## The "Terrible" Two's

Terrible is such a strong word, how about the "Transitional Two's?" It's a time of social adjustment every two year old will experience. Therefore, a group of two year old's can present quite a challenge to the (very brave) party host.

A great party for a two year old would be a family outing to their favorite place. Make it memorable by presenting them with a special souvenir and a dessert with candles. Don't forget to sing "Happy Birthday!"

## Three Year Old's

Three year old's can be an unpredictable crowd. Some three's are social, some are as mature as four year old's, while others are still experiencing the "Transitional Two's." For this reason, I recommend parties that allow the children to do things at their own pace.

Great parties for three year old's would consist of free play activities. Consider a wading pool party, a sand box social or a collection of creative arts and crafts projects.

# Let the Fun Begin...

The games and activities in this book aren't just for birthday parties. Introduce these games and activities on any occasion for fun and entertainment.

Barbecues
Beach Parties
Camp-Outs
Church Socials
Classroom Activities
Company Picnics
Family Activities
Family Reunions
Fund-Raising Activities
Homeschools
Preschools
Rainy Days
School Carnivals
Sick in Bed
Slumber Parties
Travel (*photocopy and simple art projects*)
Youth Group Meetings

For fun at Wedding Showers, try these games and activities:

At the Drive In (*for nostalgia*)
Bookmarked (*use prize winning option for a door prize*)
Dishpan Derby (*present gift certificate to spouse*)
Flip Your Lids (*to win movie tickets*)
Funcastle Maze (*help toad find the castle and become a prince*)
Penny Loafers (*wedding year instead of birth year*)
Puzzle Prizes (*everybody wins*)
Quick Draw 101 (*draw bride in her wedding gown*)
Shake, Rattle and Roll (*to get everyone on their feet*)
(His) Smelly Gym Socks (*who wants to do the laundry?*)
Tabletop Shuffleboard (*great for couples' showers*)
Wooden Spoon Golf (*anyone for miniature golf?*)

# Arrival Activities

An arrival activity is recommended to keep the children entertained until all of the guests arrive. A handmade craft will ease the children into the party atmosphere. Welcome the children to join in as soon as they arrive and let them know they're just in time for the games and excitement planned for the party. Their works of art will create a special and inexpensive favor for each to take home. Most of all, it will bring a priceless gleam to their eyes when they happily announce "I made it myself."

Remember to check the label before you purchase glue, paints, marking pens or crayons to be sure they are non-toxic and washable. If a child is to assist you in cutting materials for preparation, supply children's safety scissors for them to use.

# BASEBALL CARDS

**For Ages:** 4 to 12

**Time:** 15 minutes

## Materials Needed

1 POLAROID® instant camera (borrow or rent)
1 POLAROID® snapshot per guest plus a few extras
baseball props (baseball, mitt, cap, bat, jersey)
1 ball point pen per child
1  4" x 6" adhesive label per 2 children

## Preparation

Before the party - cut 4" x 6" adhesive labels in half vertically for 2 labels, 2" x 3" each. You will need one 2" x 3" adhesive label per child.

Before you begin - designate one helper to assist the child being photographed with the props and another helper to assist the child on deck (next to be photographed).

## How to Make

Photograph each child with the baseball props as they arrive. The children will enjoy watching the picture develop before their eyes. Encourage them to show the snapshots to one another to compare batting or catching stances. Try to snap the pictures as quickly as possible to avoid time delays.

Seat the children after all have been photographed. Hand out one ball point pen and one 2" x 3" adhesive label to each child. Ask them to list the following: name, date of birth, school, favorite movie and television show, hobby, pet's name and favorite baseball team.

When all of the statistics are recorded, help the children adhere the labels to the back of their POLAROID® snapshot. Place the label right-side up for a personalized baseball card.

## Sport Card Option

This can be a sport card of any kind. If your child is a basketball, football, hockey or soccer enthusiast, change the props and follow the directions in "How to Make."

# BOOKMARKS

**For Ages:** 4 to 12

**Time:** 15 minutes

### Materials Needed

2  4" x 6" index cards per child
scissors (for preparation only)
color marking pens
stickers

### Preparation

Before the party - cut 4" x 6" index cards in half, horizontally, for an easy to design bookmark measuring 2" x 6". Prepare 4 bookmarks per child.

Before you begin - hand out 4 bookmarks and 1 sheet of stickers to each child. Supply color marking pens for the children to share.

### How to Make

The children can create beautiful bookmarks with the stickers and color marking pens.

# CANVAS PAINTING FOR STARVING ARTISTS

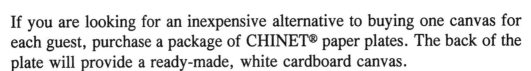

**For Ages:** 2 to 12

**Time:** 15 minutes

## Materials Needed

If you are looking for an inexpensive alternative to buying one canvas for each guest, purchase a package of CHINET® paper plates. The back of the plate will provide a ready-made, white cardboard canvas.

1 CHINET® paper plate per child
poster paints or water colors
1 paintbrush per child
1 fine point marking pen
empty yogurt cups with water to rinse brushes
paper towels

## Preparation

Before the party - be sure the package count will supply at least one plate per child and a few extras.

Before you begin - set the work table with a water cup, a paper towel (to dry the brush after rinsing), "a canvas" and a paint brush for each child. Supply paints for the children to share.

## How to Make

The children will paint a masterpiece on their "canvas" and set it aside to dry. At the end of the party, the children may sign their works of art with a fine point marking pen.

# CRAYON RUBBINGS

**For Ages:** 5 to 12

**Time:** 15 minutes

## Materials Needed

1 to 4 pieces of plain white paper per child
crayons
stencils and tracing shapes
   or an assortment of flat household items: coins, refrigerator magnets,
   combs, barrettes, keys, large paper clips, etc. (at least one per child)

## Preparation

Before the party - none.

Before you begin - give each child at least one piece of paper. Supply crayons and rubbing materials for the children to share.

## How to Make

Place the piece of paper over one stencil, tracing shape or household item. Rub the paper with the crayon to highlight the raised elements of the object. Share the items to make a variety of crayon rubbing designs.

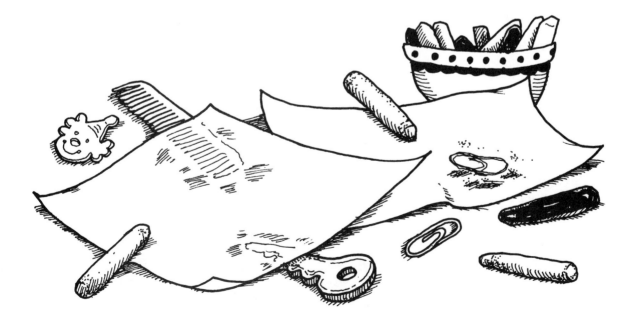

# DESIGN A STAMP & ENVELOPE FAVOR KEEPER

**For Ages:** 3 to 12

**Time:** 20 minutes

## Materials Needed

1 large white adhesive label per child
1 large mailing envelope per child
fine point color marking pens or color pencils

## Preparation

Before the party - draw an outline of a stamp on each adhesive label. Follow the easy step-by-step instructions on the opposite page.

Before you begin - hand out one outlined adhesive label to each child. Supply color marking pens or pencils for the children to share. Hold the envelopes until after the stamps are complete.

## How to Make

The children can design a stamp within the drawn outline. Remind them to include how much they think their stamp should cost (the value of the stamp). When the pictures are complete, hand out one envelope per child so they may adhere their stamp to the upper right hand corner of a large mailing envelope. Each child will have a package for collecting favors at the party.

## Special Touches

The older children can address the envelopes to themselves and write the birthday child's name and address as the sender.

Purchase a fun stamp and ink pad to have the birthday child "postmark" each envelope as your guests leave. This will give the birthday child an opportunity to say "thank you for coming to my party."

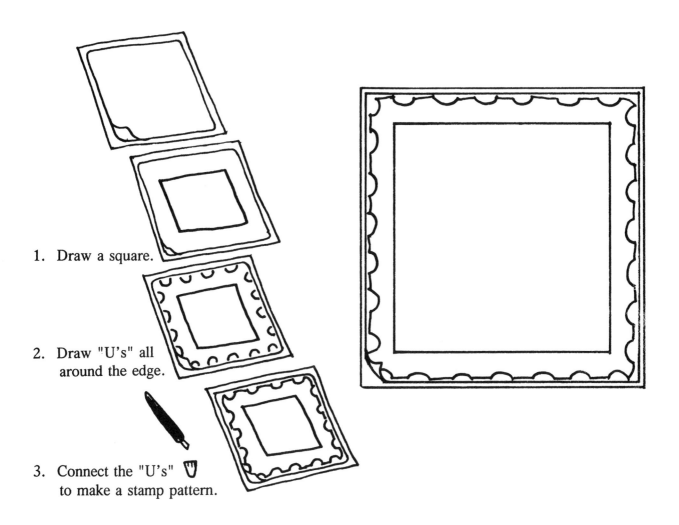

1. Draw a square.

2. Draw "U's" all around the edge.

3. Connect the "U's" to make a stamp pattern.

# LUNCH SACK FAVOR KEEPER

**For Ages:** 2 to 12

**Time:** 15 minutes

## Materials Needed

1 paper lunch sack per child
crayons (for toddlers)
color marking pens
stickers

## Preparation

Before the party - Write the children's names on their lunch sacks.

Before you begin - hand out one sheet of stickers with a personalized lunch sack to each child. Supply crayons or color marking pens for the children to share.

## How to Make

The children may design their personalized lunch sack favor keepers with the art supplies you provide.

## Creative Option

Sponge paint designs sprinkled with glitter.

# NAMEPLATES

**For Ages:** 4 to 12

**Time:** 15 minutes

## Materials Needed

3 adhesive labels or blank name tags per child
color marking pens or pencils
1 black ink or marking pen

## Preparation

Before the party - write on each label with a black ink or marking pen "This belongs to:" with a line drawn underneath to fill in the name of the child. Prepare 3 labels or name tags per child.

Before you begin - hand out 3 labels per child. Supply color marking pens or pencils for the children to share.

## How to Make

The children can fill in their name and design the border for personalized nameplates to adorn their favorite things at home: lunch boxes, folders, pencil boxes, storage containers, toys and books.

# PATCHWORK TURTLE

**For Ages:** 2 to 10

**Time:** 15 minutes

## Materials Needed

1 green card stock copy of the turtle per child
fabric remnants
several bottles of white, non-toxic glue
scissors (for preparation only)

## Preparation

Before the party - ask a local quick printer to copy the illustration onto green card stock, one per child and a few extras (less than 20 cents each). If they have any reservations, show them the permission to copy notice on the page preceding "Acknowledgements."
  Cut at least 20 one inch squares of fabric for each child.

Before you begin - write the children's names on their patchwork turtles to avoid mix-ups. Hand out one card stock turtle to each child. Supply the fabric squares and glue for the children to share.

## How to Make

The children can create a patchwork quilt on the turtle's back by mounting the squares of material with the white glue.

## Special Touches

Add buttons for eyes and top off each turtle's head with a bow or a hat.

## Coloring Option

Design a patchwork quilt with crayons, color pencils or marking pens.

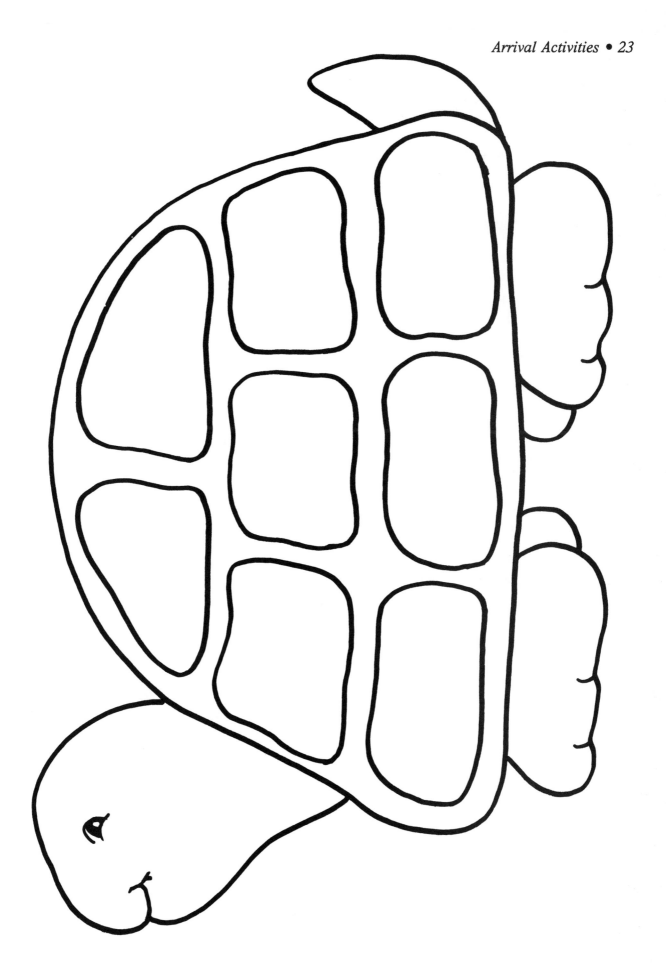

# TILE MOSAICS

**For Ages:** 4 to 12

**Time:** 15 minutes

## Materials Needed

1 large white posterboard
a selection of uncooked beans,
  macaroni, corn, dry cereal,
  hard candies (colorful items)
several bottles of white, non-toxic glue
scissors (for preparation only)

## Preparation

Before the party - cut one 6-inch square for each child from the white posterboard. Place the food items in separate bowls.

Before you begin - hand out one "tile" to each child. Supply the mosaic materials and glue for the children to share.

## How to Make

The children can design "mosaic tiles" by mounting the pieces of food on the posterboard with glue.

# *Relays*

Before you add a relay race to your game line-up, consider these factors: Is there enough space on carpeting or lawn to run the relay and are the guests 5 years of age or older? If you don't have the surface for safe landings and can't keep the little ones from being trampled in a fast-paced race, choose Flapjack Frenzy.

Each relay requires two equal teams and two turnaround points. The host should divide the children into teams to make it a fair race and to avoid hurt feelings that can result when choosing by team captains. If the teams are uneven, ask a sibling or helper to fill in or designate a child to run twice. Turnaround points can be any of the following: Plastic trash cans, chairs, empty boxes, parents or siblings; any two items that are similar and safe. Make sure they are spaced evenly from the start line and far enough apart to avoid opposing team member collisions.

For relay races on lawn choose an area that is free from sprinklers, sticks or other dangerous objects. Keep in mind that while relay races can be exciting and fun for the children, they can also be dangerous if not well planned and properly supervised.

# BALL BOY/GIRL RELAY

**For Ages:** 5 to 12

**Time:** 3 minutes

## Materials Needed

plenty of baseballs, softballs, tennis balls, etc.
a supply of large t-shirts

## Preparation

Before the party - have a supply of clean, large t-shirts ready to use.

Before you play - determine who will need a large t-shirt. Most boys will be wearing a suitable t-shirt. The girls wearing a dress or short blouse will need to put on a large t-shirt over their clothes.

Set up the turnaround points and divide the children into two teams. Divide the balls equally and place them on the ground in front of the first runners for each team.

## Introducing the Relay

"You are the new ball boys and girls for your favorite baseball team. Your job is to get all of the baseballs off the field as fast as you can."

## How to Play

The first runner in line will pick up the balls and place them in their t-shirt, like a kangaroo's pouch. Carry the balls around the turnaround point without spilling any of the balls. If any are dropped, they must be replaced before continuing the race. Dump the balls into the next runner's t-shirt (or kangaroo's pouch) and continue the relay until each ball boy and girl has carried the balls "off the field." The team that finishes first wins.

**Prizes:** Baseball prizes such as erasers, pencils, key chains or play baseballs.

**Favors:** Cut pennant flag shapes from a felt square and hot glue to an unsharpened pencil just below the eraser. Give one to each child for an inexpensive and fun favor.

# DOUBLE SCOOP RELAY

**For Ages:** 5 to 12

**Time:** 5 minutes

## Materials Needed

1 or 2 packages of plain cake ice cream cones
  (1 cone per child)
2 large craft poms or large marshmallows per child
2 plastic bowls
2 ice cream scoops or spoons
2 chairs

## Preparation

Before the party - none.

Before you play - set up two chairs facing the relay teams as the turnaround points. Place a spoon and a dish of "ice cream" (2 craft poms or large marshmallows per team member) on each chair. For example: For 8 runners, 2 teams of 4 runners, you will need 8 scoops of "ice cream" in each dish. Divide the children into two teams and give each child a cone.

## Introducing the Relay

"Double your scoop and run, run, run
 in this relay that's gallons of fun."

## How to Play

The first runner for each team will run to the chair, scoop two craft poms or marshmallows into their cone with the spoon and return to their team while trying not to drop any of the scoops. If one is dropped they must pick it up where it fell, replace it and continue the race. Tag the next runner in line so they can run to the dish of "ice cream" and fill their own cone with a "double scoop." The winning team is the first team to have all of their cones filled with two scoops of "ice cream."

**Prizes:** Ice cream parlor or store gift certificates.

**Favors:** Everyone keeps the sugar cone and craft poms or marshmallows.

# EARLY BIRD RELAY

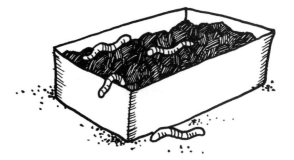

**For Ages:** 5 to 12

**Time:** 3 minutes

## Materials Needed

2 empty shoe boxes
2 straw paper plate holders
1 small bag of potting soil
1 gummy worm per child

## Preparation

Before the party - fill each shoe box with soil and 1 gummy worm per team member. For example: For 8 runners you will need 4 gummy worms in each box. Bury the worms below the surface.

Before you play - set up a straw paper plate as the turnaround point for each team. Divide the children into two teams. Place the shoe boxes in front of the first runner for each team.

## Introducing the Relay

"The early birds will get the worms first and win the relay."

## How to Play

The first runner for each team will unearth a worm, carry it to the turnaround point and drop it in the "bird's nest" (straw paper plate holder), return to their team and tag the next runner. The first team to fill their "bird's nest" with "worms" will win the relay.

**Prizes:** Two gummy worms each for the "early birds" and one gummy worm each for the "late birds" or runners-up.

**Favors:** Bird whistles.

# FLAPJACK FRENZY

**For Ages:** 4 to 12

**Time:** 3 minutes

## Materials Needed

2 frying pans of equal size
2 pancake turners or regular spatulas
2 decorative square hot pads

## Preparation

Before the party - none.

Before you play - divide the children into two teams. Line up the children and have the opposing teams face one another. Seat the children with plenty of space, or elbow room, between them.

Give the first child on each team the frying pan, hot pad "flapjack" and the spatula.

## Introducing the Relay

"Order's up for flapjacks!"

## How to Play

The first child in each line must flip the "flapjack" into the air with the spatula and land it in the frying pan. After it lands in the frying pan, they can pass all of the items to the next player in line. Continue until the frying pan, "flapjack" and spatula reaches the last team member and they win the relay with their final successful flip. Everyone must remain seated during the relay.

It may take a while to accomplish this feat, but the children will enjoy the hot pads frantically flipping through the air. By facing one another, the teams can see how they are faring in the race. The first team to have each child successfully flip a hot pad "flapjack" into the frying pan wins.

**Prizes and Favors:** This game is fast and furious so it may be difficult to keep track of who's winning after a few rounds (yes, they will want to play this one again and again). Award everyone the same prize or favor for playing the game: Snack size food storage containers, kitchen magnets or recipes for kids written on index cards (add stickers and drawings to decorate).

# GALAXY RELAY

**For Ages:** 5 to 7

**Time:** 3 minutes

## Materials Needed

A side of a tent, wall or fence
1 sheet of construction paper per 4 children
scissors (for preparation only)
masking tape
1 pen or pencil

## Preparation

Before the party - cut star shapes from the construction paper and write the children's names on them, one per star. If there is an uneven number of players, prepare a star for yourself or an adult helper to run the relay. Tape the stars randomly on the side of a tent, wall or fence to appear as a galaxy.

Before you play - divide the children into two teams.

## Introducing the Relay

"A star has been named after each one of you. Find your star in the 'galaxy' and bring it back to Earth."

## How to Play

The first runner in each line will run to the "galaxy" and find the star that was named after them, grab the star and return to tag the next runner on their team. The first team to retrieve all of their personalized stars from the "galaxy" wins.

## Special Touch

Use glow-in-the-dark stars with names written in permanent marking pen and play at dusk.

**Prizes:** Star stickers.

**Favors:** Each child keeps the star that was named after them.

# HOT CHILI PEPPER CHASE

**For Ages:** 5 to 12

**Time:** 3 minutes

## Materials Needed

2 oven mitts
2 chili peppers - use red or green bell peppers
   in case one of the children decide to take a bite of the "hot chili pepper"

## Preparation

Before the party - none.

Before you play - set up the turnaround points and divide the children into two teams.

## Introducing the Relay

"Hand over those hot chili peppers to the cooks on your team with a mitt and keep your cool."

## How to Play

The first person on each team will be given an oven mitt to wear and a "hot chili pepper" to hold in the same hand. Carry the "hot chili pepper" to the turnaround point and back to hand off the oven mitt and "hot chili pepper" to the next runner. When your teammate has the oven mitt and the "hot chili pepper" in hand he can continue the chase. The first team to finish the "hot chili pepper chase" will be the winning team.

**Prizes:** Cinnamon or fire flavored candies or treats.

**Favors:** Make "hot chili pepper" bookmarks out of green and red construction paper for each child.

# MOUSETRAP GETAWAY

**For Ages:** 5 to 9

**Time:** 2 minutes

## Materials Needed

2 large yellow sponges

## Preparation

Before the party - none.

Before you play - set up the turnaround points and divide the children into two teams.

## Introducing the Relay

"You are the mice that have just stolen the cheese from the mousetrap." Clap your hands loudly and say "Snap! It was a very narrow escape." "Now, try to escape the cat that's on your tail with the piece of cheese (sponge) trapped between your knees."

## How to Play

The first "mouse" in line is to run and circle the turnaround point with the "cheese" between their knees, return to their team and pass the "cheese" with their "paws" to the next "mouse" in line to continue the race. The team to finish the relay first has escaped the "cat" and wins a prize.

**Prizes:** Cheese flavored snacks.

**Favors:** Cat stickers.

# "SUPER" MARKET RELAY

**For Ages:** 5 to 12

**Time:** 3 minutes

## Materials Needed

2 large, brown paper grocery bags
2 like grocery items per pair of children
  For example: check your pantry or refrigerator for two boxes of cereal, two rolls of paper towels, two empty two-liter soda bottles, two pieces of fruit, two microwave popcorn packages, etc. Anything you have two of that won't break any toes when dropped (no cans, glass jars or bottles). For every two children on your guest list you will need a matching pair of grocery items.

## Preparation

Before the party - collect the grocery items to be used in the relay. Keep them in each grocery bag until time to play.

Before you play - divide the children into two teams and give each 1st runner the same item, each 2nd runner the same item, etc. Set up the empty grocery bags as the turnaround points.

## Introducing the Relay

"Paper or Plastic? Paper please, to see if you can pack these groceries with ease."

## How to Play

The first runner will place his item in the grocery bag and return to tag the next runner in line. Each runner will try to neatly pack their item in the grocery bag as quickly as possible. When the first team finishes, wait and let the second team complete the relay.

After the relay is over, announce the winning team is the team that has packed the groceries the neatest. Award both teams the same prize, but allow the neatest team to choose first.

## Game Tip

To add some good humor to the game, give the first runners in line the small or fruit items and the last few runners in line the larger or heavier items. The children will try to rearrange the items to make them fit or have fun trying. The older children will enjoy the challenge.

**Prizes:** Allow the winning team to choose first from an assortment of snack size groceries such as cereal, granola bars, fruit snacks, potato chips, crackers and cookies.

**Favors:** Before the relay, hand out personalized name tags with the name of a local grocery store written above each child's name.

# TENNIS ELBOW RELAY

**For Ages:** 5 to 12

**Time:** 3 minutes

**Materials Needed**

2 or 4 tennis balls

**Preparation**

Before the party - none.

Before you play - set up the turnaround points and divide the children into two teams.

**Introducing the Relay**

"Tennis Elbow is contagious in this relay as you pass it along to your teammate to win the match."

**How to Play**

Place the tennis ball inside one elbow of the first runner on each team. If playing with four tennis balls, the first runners will each have two "tennis elbows." The runner must circle the turnaround point and hand off the tennis ball(s) to the next teammate's elbow without using their hands. When they've accomplished the hand-off, the race continues. If a tennis ball is dropped during the course of the relay, it must be picked up at the point where it fell, placed in the elbow and the race continued. The team of "tennis elbows" to finish the relay first wins.

**Prizes:** Gold medals (chocolate coins) for the "WimbleElbow" winners and silver medals (flat cookies or frozen juice can lids wrapped in foil) for the runners-up.

**Favors:** Serve lemon sandwich cookies with tennis ball seams drawn in yellow or white with a fine-tipped tube of frosting.

# *Everybody Wins*

Games should be fun for everyone, not just the select few that are lucky enough to win a prize. The money spent on a few nice gifts can be used to buy several favors for each child on the guest list. If you purchase items in bulk from discount party and retail stores or mail order catalogs, you save money and have enough prizes for everyone. Use leftover favors for Easter basket surprises, Christmas stocking stuffers, safe Halloween hand-outs, sibling's parties or give to your favorite teacher for classroom rewards.

Try one of these prize winning suggestions for the games on your list:

 Instead of saving all the best favors for the end of the party, hand them out after each game. Select a particular favor for each game and allow the winner to choose first. Hand out the remaining favors to the runners-up. Everyone wins just for playing the game. Provide a personalized favor keeper for each child to hold their winnings.

 Provide one unwrapped prize per child. Hide the prizes in a box away from the party area. Hand out tickets after each game, 2 for the winner and 1 for each runner-up. Set up personalized lunch sacks to hold the tickets while they play. At the end of the games, have the children count their tickets and announce the total. The child with the most tickets will be first to select one prize from the box. One at a time, call upon each child according to the number of tickets collected. Everyone will receive a prize for participating in the games.

Your party will be a huge success when you use one of these suggestions or host at least one game from "Everybody Wins." The thrill and excitement of winning will overflow into the festivities, making it a joyous occasion for all who attend.

# AT THE DRIVE-IN

**For Ages:** 4 to 12

**Time:** 5 minutes

## Materials Needed

1 small toy car per child
  (various makes and colors)
1 small posterboard
1 black marking pen
1 candy prize per child
1 small box (optional)

## Preparation

Before the party - place a small box or draw a square in the center of the posterboard and label it "Snack Bar." Draw parking spaces for the toy cars with the marking pen on the posterboard around the snack bar. Number the spaces 1 through the number of children. Number the candies to correspond with the parking spaces.

Before you play - place the posterboard "drive-in movie theater" on the floor. Give each child one toy car to park at the "drive-in."

## Introducing the Game

"We're going to the drive-in theater. Remember the color and design of your car and where you parked so you won't get lost on the way back from the snack bar."

## How to Play

Each child will park their car in a numbered square on the posterboard. One at a time, call on the children to pick up their car and announce the number written within the parking space. Award the piece of "snack bar" candy that corresponds to their parking space number. Continue until everyone receives their prize from the "snack bar."

**Prizes:** Candy.

**Favors:** Everyone can keep their toy car.

# CAT AND MOUSE

**For Ages:** 2 to 10

**Time:** 8 minutes

## Materials Needed

1 medium to large cardboard box with a lid
scissors or box knife (for preparation only)
1 small wrapped prize per child

## Preparation

Before the party - cut away a mouse hole from the box, just large enough for a child's hand to fit into easily. Place one wrapped prize into the box for each child and close the lid.

Before you play - none.

## Introducing the Game

Announce to the children they will be cats for this game and you need to hear their best meow. One at a time, call on the children to meow and purr like a cat. Next, tell them that a mouse in the house has taken all of the prizes for this game and hidden them in the wall.

## How to Play

The "cats" (children) will take turns reaching into the "mouse hole" with one "paw" (hand) to retrieve a prize from the "mouse."

## Surprise Option

If you have a toy mouse, put it in the box for an added surprise. The first one to find the mouse will jump, laugh and giggle along with everyone else. Return the mouse to his house and try for a prize. The children will follow suit and try to catch the mouse. This option is recommended for children over 6 years of age who won't be alarmed or upset by an unexpected, surprise toy mouse.

**Prizes:** Gifts that will fit in the palm of a child's hand; prism scopes, beanbag balls and yoyos.

# MAGIC CARPET SWEEP

**For Ages:** 2 to 10

**Time:** 5 minutes

## Materials Needed

1 kitchen towel
  or washcloth per child
1 small unwrapped prize per child

## Preparation

Before the party - none.

Before you play - lay the kitchen towels or washcloths on the floor like rugs or "magic carpets."

## Introducing the Game

"These are the magic carpets I had flown in especially for the party. They are magic because prizes will mysteriously appear under the carpets after you hide your eyes."

## How to Play

Have the children turn away from the "magic carpets" or leave the room for a moment while you "sweep" prizes under the "rugs." When you have finished placing one prize under each towel or washcloth they can turn around or return to the playing area. Call on the children one at a time to stand up and select a "magic carpet." There is no peeking allowed. When they've made their decision they can lift the "magic carpet" to reveal their prize.

**Prizes:** Save leftover favors from previous parties for a variety of inexpensive gifts.

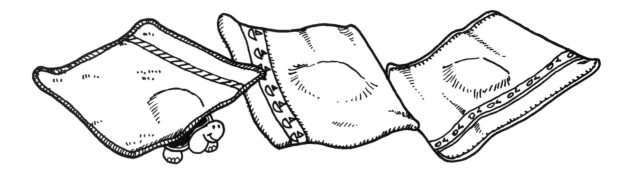

# MOON WALKERS

**For Ages:** 4 to 10

**Time:** 10 minutes

## Materials Needed

a moon's surface:
  1 foam support mattress (crater side up)
  or 1 exercise mat or 1 yellow or beige blanket
1 small prize per child
aluminum foil

## Preparation

Before the party - wrap one small prize in aluminum foil for each child.

Before you play - set up the mattress, mat or blanket (fold blanket lengthwise once or twice). Scatter the wrapped moon rock prizes along the path of the "moon's surface." Have the children take off their shoes to "walk on the moon."

## Introducing the Game

"You are astronauts that have been sent to the moon on a very special mission. As you walk the moon's surface, you must collect one moon rock to bring back to earth."

## How to Play

An adult helper will spot each child as they walk across the "moon," one at a time. Each "moon walker" will bend down to collect one "moon rock" along the path of their "star trek." When all of your "astronauts" have returned to earth, they may unwrap their "moon rock" for a prize.

**Prizes:** Glow-in-the-dark prizes such as bounce balls, play putty or stars.

# PENNY LOAFERS

**For Ages:** 4 to 12

**Time:** 5 minutes to introduce the game and place the penny in a shoe, 5 minutes to claim prizes later in the party.

## Materials Needed

1 penny per child
   include 1 penny dated 1950 to 1959 (for nostalgia) or 1 penny that features the guest of honor's birth year

## Preparation

Before the party - place the game pennies in a jar or coin bank.

Before you play - while your guests are busy with the arrival activity, count your pennies again to be sure you have only one per child and that you have included the winning penny.

## Introducing the Game

"Penny loafers were one of the footwear fads of the fifties, along with saddle shoes. A penny was placed in the top slot of each leather upper. This is why they were called penny loafers. Let's put on our penny loafers to wear at the party."

## How to Play

Greet each guest with the shake of the jar or bank until a penny falls into their hand. Instruct the children to put the penny in their shoe, so everyone will be wearing "penny loafers" at the party.

Announce to the children the penny must remain in their shoe until you play the game a little later.

At an appropriate time, as gifts are gathered for opening or at a break in the party action, ask the children to remove the penny from their shoes. Announce the winning year and award the rightful "penny loafer" owner a prize.

**Prizes:** The winning penny buys a gumball bank, coin bank or small bag of gumballs to tie into the penny theme.

**Favors:** Everyone can "buy" a gumball or penny candy from the host with the game penny from their shoe.

## Everybody Wins Option

Select pennies with various years. Write each year on a corresponding wrapped gift. Call out the dates, one at a time, to match the prizes to the pennies.

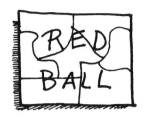

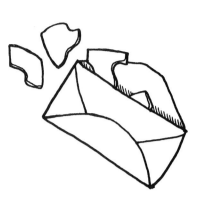

# PUZZLE PRIZES

**For Ages:** 5 to 12

**Time:** 12 minutes

## Materials Needed

1 previous year wall calendar
   for each 12 children or 1
   old greeting card per child
several rolls of transparent tape
1 envelope per child
1 prize per child
1 marking pen
1 pencil
scissors (for preparation only)

## Preparation

Before the party - tear the picture calendar pages from the binding or cut the greeting cards at the fold. On the back of each picture write the name of one prize in large, bold letters with the marking pen. Draw a simple jigsaw puzzle pattern on the back of each picture in pencil. Cut and insert the pieces of the puzzle into an envelope and seal. You will need one puzzle per envelope, per child.

Before you play - hand out one envelope containing a puzzle to each child.

## Introducing the Game

"Piece together a puzzle to discover a prize."

## How to Play

Ask the children to open their envelopes and put together the puzzle inside. When it's complete, use only enough transparent tape to hold the pieces in place. Have the children turn over their completed puzzle to reveal the name of the prize written on the back. Award the prizes accordingly.

**Prizes:** Activity books, school or art supplies, key chains and sticker albums.

# SMELLY GYM SOCKS

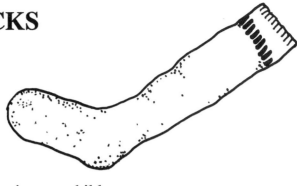

**For Ages:** 4 to 12

**Time:** 3 minutes

## Materials Needed

1 large sport sock per child
1 small unbreakable, lightweight prize per child
prerecorded music or radio

## Preparation

Before the party - drop one prize into a sock, roll up the sock starting at the toe and fold over the top to make a ball. Prepare one prize winning sock per child.

Before you play - hand out one "smelly gym sock" to each child. Do not announce there is a prize inside the sock until after the game.

## Introducing the Game

"Keep those smelly gym socks away from me!"

## How to Play

As the music plays the children will toss the "smelly gym socks" to one another, trying to keep them inside of the circle. When the music stops, make sure each child is holding only one "smelly gym sock." Announce to the children they may open their "smelly gym sock" for a prize.

**Prizes:** Lightweight prizes that will fit into the toe of a sock: snack size candies, miniature yoyos and soft plastic toys.

# SURPRISE BOULDER PIÑATA

**For Ages:** 2 to 8

**Time:** 6 minutes

## Materials Needed

1 large brown paper grocery bag
2 plastic grocery bags
1 newspaper
clear packaging tape
1 round laundry basket
1 resealable sandwich bag per child
piñata treats and favors

## Preparation

Before the party - fill the sandwich bags with an equal amount of treats and small favors. Make sure they are sealed securely or tied with a ribbon. Fill the brown paper bag with crumpled newspapers and one piñata treat bag per child (be sure to include a bag for the birthday child). Close the brown paper bag and seal with clear packaging tape. Place inside one plastic bag (turn inside out to hide store logo) and tie the ends. Put inside the second plastic bag and tie the ends to double bag. Seal with clear packaging tape.

Before you play - Do not at any time announce that the boulder is a piñata, or you will give away the surprise. Refer to the game as "Boulder Basketball."

## Introducing the Game

"How about a game of boulder basketball? No dribbling or you might break your toe."

## How to Play

The children will line up and take turns tossing the "boulder" into the laundry basket. Every child will win with either a nonchalant assist by you or by standing close enough to the basket to succeed.

Reward all participants after the game by allowing the birthday child to tear into the "boulder" and give each guest a piñata favor bag.

This new piñata activity will avoid injuries and give everyone an equal amount of treats.

**\*Safety Tip:** If small children are expected to attend the party, prepare bags especially for them with fruit snacks, animal crackers and other special treats that won't present a choking hazard.

**Piñata Treats and Favors:** Assorted candies, stickers, lightweight plastic toys, miniature books, note pads or erasers.

# TRAPPED IN TAR

**For Ages:** 4 to 6

**Time:** 12 minutes

## Materials Needed

2 to 3 pounds of dry uncooked black beans
1 package of small, bone-shape dog biscuits
1 plastic toy dinosaur per child
1 large unbreakable bowl
1 non-toxic, fine point marking pen

## Preparation

Before the party - write a dinosaur species on the back of each bone, one name to correspond with each of the toy dinosaurs. For example: if you have 3 toy Stegosaurus', make 3 Stegosaurus bones, 2 Tyrannosaurs, make 2 T-Rex bones, etc. Place the bones in the bottom of the bowl and cover with black beans. Hide the bowl in a secret place away from the party area.

Before you play - none.

## Introducing the Game

"We are paleontologists in search of the tar pits from long ago. The dinosaurs were trapped in the sticky stuff and their bones were preserved for us to study today. Follow me to see if we can find a tar pit full of bones."

## How to Play

Play "Follow the Leader" with the birthday child in line right behind you. Lead the children on a silly safari that will bring them to the "tar pit." Let the birthday child discover the "tar pit" and pull it out for all to see. One at a time, each paleontologist will unearth a bone by reaching into the "tar pit." After each child has discovered one bone, match the name to the same species of toy dinosaur. Collect the bone and award the dinosaur to the child.

**\*Pet Safety Tip:** Throw away the bones with the ink writing.

**Prizes:** Plastic toy dinosaurs.

**Favors:** The remaining "dinosaur" bones from the package of dog biscuits with no ink writing.

## *Tossing Games*

Tossing games, like the ones played at carnivals, are a favorite at parties. For the children, it's a game of chance they'll want to play again and again. For the parents, it's a better alternative to the amusement park games that can cost $1.00 to $2.00 per play.

If you announce to the children that all of them will receive a favor just for participating, it will take away the pressure and allow them to have more fun. Be sure to cheer them on and lead everyone in applause for each child's efforts. Award the favors after everyone has taken their turn.

If you'd like to keep a record and determine a winner, be prepared for ties. Always hold a toss-off or award all tie winners. Selecting a number from 1 to 10 as a tiebreaker is very disappointing to the children who miss the draw.

# COCOON CATCH

**For Ages:** 4 to 12

**Time:** 5 minutes

## Materials Needed

3 peanuts in the shell
1 butterfly net or large fish net (from the pet store)

## Preparation

Before the party - none.

Before you play - have the children form a single file line facing the host who will be holding the net.

## Introducing the Game

"Give the creatures in these cocoons early flying lessons by tossing them into the butterfly net."

## How to Play

Each child will take 3 turns to toss a peanut "cocoon," one at a time, into the butterfly net. See how many "cocoons" the net keeper can catch.

After the first child in line tosses the "cocoons," let them be the net keeper for the next player. They'll enjoy catching the "cocoons" as much as tossing them. Make sure each child has a turn to catch as well as toss.

## Game Tip

If you expect more than eight guests, buy another net and host two lines so the children won't have to wait so long for their turns.

**\*Safety Tip:** As with any game or activity that involves small objects or food items that will present a choking hazard, be careful to keep these items out of the reach of infants, toddlers and/or pets.

**Favors:** Butterfly stickers to decorate a resealable sandwich bag full of "cocoons" (peanuts).

# DISHPAN DERBY

**For Ages:** 2 to 8

**Time:** 3 minutes

**Materials Needed**

1 dish drainer
3 paper cups

## Preparation

Before the party - none.

Before you play - designate a throw line and have the children form a single file line behind it. Set up the dish drainer as the target (gauge distance according to age and ability).

## Introducing the Game

"We're going to air dry these dishes by tossing them through the air and into the dish drainer."

## How to Play

Each child will have a turn to toss 3 cups, one at a time, into the dish drainer.

**Favors:** Copy the gift certificate on this page to award to each "dish dryer." Tell them to present it to their favorite dishwasher as a special gift. Remind them not to toss the dishes when they help.

# FLIP YOUR LIDS

**For Ages:** 4 to 12

**Time:** 4 minutes

## Materials Needed

3 large beverage lids
1 large popcorn bucket

## Preparation

Before the party - save 3 large beverage lids from fast food restaurant visits (rinse and dry). Save 1 large popcorn bucket from a trip to the movies, no butter on this one.

Before you play - designate a throw line and have the children form a single file line behind it. Set up the popcorn bucket as the target (gauge distance according to age and ability).

## Introducing the Game

"Since you're not allowed to send your soda lids sailing towards the big screen, go ahead and flip your lids at this popcorn bucket."

## How to Play

Each child will have a turn to toss 3 beverage lids, one at a time, into the popcorn bucket.

## Game Tip

Provide a backboard for rebound shots by placing the popcorn bucket in front of a wall.

**Favors:** Small flying discs.

# MAN OVERBOARD

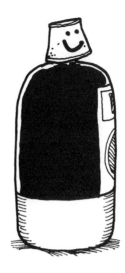

**For Ages:** 2 to 12

**Time:** 3 minutes

## Materials Needed

1 to 3 toddler size swim rings
1 full two-liter bottle of soda

## Preparation

Before the party - inflate the swim ring(s).

Before you play - designate a throw line and have the children form a single file line behind it. Set up the two-liter bottle as the target (gauge distance according to age and ability).

## Introducing the Game

"Your first mate has just fallen overboard. Toss him a lifesaving ring to rescue him from the sea."

## How to Play

Each child will have a turn to toss a swim ring 3 times to the "man overboard." Try to land the swim ring around the two-liter bottle.

## Special Touch:

Draw a face on an upside-down paper cup and tape it to the top of the two-liter bottle to give your "man overboard" character.

**Favors:** Hot glue a length of wide ribbon to a frozen juice can lid for a "medal" necklace and award one to each child.

# MARSHMALLOW MOON ROCK TOSS

**For Ages:** 3 to 12

**Time:** 4 minutes

## Materials Needed

1 package of large marshmallows
8 to 12 thin paper dessert bowls
1 large white posterboard
scissors (for preparation only)
transparent or masking tape

## Preparation

Before the party - cut out the bottoms of 8 to 12 paper dessert bowls, leaving a rim to resemble a moon crater when turned upside down. Strategically place the overturned bowls on the posterboard and secure with tape.

Before you play - designate a throw line and have the children form a single file line behind it. Set up the "moon crater" posterboard as the target (gauge distance according to age and ability).

## Introducing the Game

"As you leave the moon's orbit, you realize you've collected too many moon rocks on this expedition. Toss some of the moon rocks back into the craters."

## How to Play

Each child will have a turn to toss 3 marshmallow "moon rocks," one at a time, into the craters.

**Favors:** An extra bag of large marshmallow "moon rocks" for snacking.

# PAPER ROUTE

**For Ages:** 4 to 12

**Time:** 5 minutes

## Materials Needed

1 door mat or cardboard box
1 section of newspaper
1 one-gallon plastic
    food storage bag
2 rubber bands

## Preparation

Before the party - fold and roll a section of newspaper small enough to fit into the food storage bag. Bind with one rubber band and place inside the plastic bag. Wrap the remainder of the bag around the newspaper and secure with another rubber band on the outside.

Before you play - designate a throw line and have the children form a single file line behind it. Set up the door mat or box as the target (gauge distance according to age and ability).

## Introducing the Game

"We all know you need good aim if you want to work on a paper route. This is your training session for the important position of paper carrier."

## How to Play

Each child will take one turn to toss the newspaper at the target. Try to land the newspaper on the door mat or in the box. Award everyone a prize for finishing the paper route.

**Favors:**  Roll up and secure with a rubber band comic books, kid's magazines or single pages from a coloring book. If the children open their favors during the party, be sure to collect the rubber bands.

# RINGS AROUND SATURN

**For Ages:** 4 to 12

**Time:** 4 minutes

**Materials Needed**

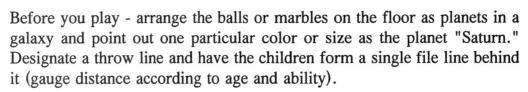

small rubber bounce balls
  or marbles
plastic bracelets

**Preparation**

Before the party - none.

Before you play - arrange the balls or marbles on the floor as planets in a galaxy and point out one particular color or size as the planet "Saturn." Designate a throw line and have the children form a single file line behind it (gauge distance according to age and ability).

## Introducing the Game

"Saturn's rings have fallen from the universe. Toss them into the galaxy to replace the rings around Saturn."

## How to Play

Each child will have a turn to toss 3 bracelets, one at a time, at the "planets." Aim for "Saturn" and try to land the bracelet completely around the ball or marble.

## Special Touch

Use different sizes to resemble the planets in the galaxy. Label or color ping pong balls if you don't have rubber bounce balls or marbles.

**\*Safety Tip:** Do not use marbles or small rubber bounce balls if infants, toddlers and/or pets are in the party area. They will present a choking hazard.

**Favors:** If the number of planets and bracelets equals the same number of guests, after the game is over let the children select one favor each from the galaxy; a "ring" or a "planet."

# THREE-RING CIRCUS

**For Ages:** 2 to 7

**Time:** 4 minutes

**Materials Needed**

3 hula hoops or
  3 round laundry baskets
3 circus theme stuffed animals
  (lion, tiger, bear, seal, elephant, dog, horse)

## Preparation

Before the party - none.

Before you play - designate a throw line and walk forward about 6 to 10 steps (gauge distance according to the ages and abilities of your guests). Place the first ring, then the second ring directly behind the first ring, and the third ring behind the second ring for three consecutive targets. Have the children form a single file line behind the designated throw line.

## Introducing the Game

"You are the ringmasters presenting the greatest three-ring circus on earth."

## How to Play

Give the first child in line one of the circus theme animals to toss into the first, or closest ring. Hand the child the second animal to try for the second ring. The third animal will be tossed into the farthest ring. When the child has accomplished this feat, they will have a "three-ring circus."

## Game Tip

If you have younger children, allow them to stand closer to the rings. It's okay to give everyone a fair chance. Games are always more fun when everybody wins.

**Favors:** Hand out frosted animal cookies to all of the children for playing the game.

# TREASURE ISLAND

**For Ages:** 4 to 12

**Time:** 5 minutes

## Materials Needed

3 to 5 pennies per child
1 small wading pool
1 styrofoam tortilla warmer lid
  or 1 flying disc, anything flat that will
  float on top of the water like an island

## Preparation

Before the party - fill the wading pool and float the "island" on top of the water.

Before you play - designate a throw line near the wading pool (gauge distance according to age and ability) and have the children form a single file line behind it.

## Introducing the Game

"Turn this desert island into a treasure island by tossing your pennies onto shore."

## How to Play

The children will pitch 3 to 5 pennies each into the wading pool. The child who lands the most pennies on "treasure island" wins.

**Favors:** Keep a record of successes and allow the winner to collect and keep all of the pennies from "treasure island." Retrieve the pennies from the water and divide them equally among the other players.

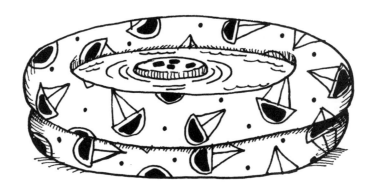

# Quiet Games

Provide a balance in your game plan by alternating quiet and active games. Quiet, circle activities work well to calm the children after a relay or active game. The sit-down games in this chapter allow the children, and you, a time to rest. By alternating quiet and active games you can maintain a desirable energy level among the children and prevent them from getting overly excited or bored.

# BOOKMARKED

**For Ages:** 3 to 12

**Time:** 5 minutes

## Materials Needed

1 bookmark per child (handmade or store bought)
1 thick storybook or dictionary
1 drawing bucket
1 small piece of paper per child
1 pencil

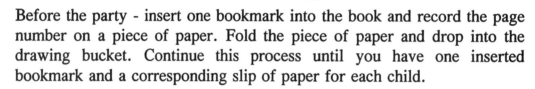

## Preparation

Before the party - insert one bookmark into the book and record the page number on a piece of paper. Fold the piece of paper and drop into the drawing bucket. Continue this process until you have one inserted bookmark and a corresponding slip of paper for each child.

Before you play - seat the children in a circle.

## Introducing the Game

"Not only have I lost my place in this book, but I can't find any of my bookmarks either, can you help me find them?"

## How to Play

The children will take turns choosing a slip of paper from the bucket. One at a time, the children will read the page number to the host who will turn to the corresponding page number in the book. The host will retrieve the bookmark and award it to the child.

## Prize Winning Option

Mark one of the bookmarks with a star or a sticker and award the child that selects the winning bookmark a prize.

**Favors:** Everyone keeps their bookmark.

# FUNNY GHOST STORIES

**For Ages:** 8 to 12

**Time:** 10 minutes

**Materials Needed**

1 small lollipop per child
1 white paper napkin per child
1 marking pen
string

## Preparation

Before the party - write the name of one ghostly character and a fun kid's place on each napkin. For example: "Frankenstein - an amusement park" or "Bride of Frankenstein - a shopping mall" or "Loch Ness Monster - a local water park." Invent one funny combination per child.

Make your ghost lollipop by placing the center of the napkin over the top of the sucker, concealing the names. Tie at the neck with string. Color the ghostly eyes and mouth with the marking pen. Make one per guest.

Before you play - seat the children in a circle. Hand out one ghostly lollipop to each child.

## Introducing the Game

"It's time to tickle your funny bones with some very funny ghost stories."

## How to Play

Tell them to untie their ghost to reveal the storytelling plot idea on the inside of the napkin. Each child will make up and share a funny ghost story if the monster were to visit the fun kid's place.

## More Fun Plot Ideas

Godzilla - Grand Canyon
Invisible Man - miniature golf course
Big Foot - bowling alley
Count Dracula - pizza arcade
The Mummy - skating rink

It's easy to create plot ideas. Make a list of monsters and match them to a fun place that might create a humorous situation if they were to visit.

# FUNNY GHOST STORIES (continued)

**Game Tip:** If the children experience stage fright, share a funny ghost story to spark their storytelling imaginations.

**Favors:** Everyone keeps the ghostly lollipop.

# HOT AND COLD TAMALE

**For Ages:** 4 to 12

**Time:** 5 minutes

## Materials Needed

1 package of HOT TAMALES®
   chewy cinnamon flavored candies
1 plastic resealable sandwich bag
1 washcloth

## Preparation

Before the party - fill the plastic sandwich bag with the candy and seal. Fold the candy inside the washcloth and wrap to resemble a tamale. Hide the tamale in an unusual place in the party area or close by.

Before you play - seat the children in a circle.

## Introducing the Game

"If you don't find this hot tamale pronto, you'll be eating a cold tamale for lunch."

## How to Play

The children will remain seated throughout the entire game. Each child will be allowed to make one guess to try and locate the hidden "tamale." When a child announces a spot you can say "warm" if they are a little close, "cold" if they are way off and "hot" if they guess the exact location. The children will take turns guessing the whereabouts of the hidden "tamale" until the exact location is revealed. The winner can retrieve the "hot tamale" and keep the red hot prize inside. You may hide as many "hot tamales" as you wish to prepare.

**\*Safety Tip:** As with any game or activity that involves small objects or food items that will present a choking hazard, be careful to keep these items out of the reach of infants, toddlers and/or pets.

**Prizes:** The winner keeps the plastic bag filled with HOT TAMALES® chewy cinnamon flavored candies.

**Favors:** Share some candy with everyone.

# MAKING THE GRADES

**For Ages:** 4 to 12

**Time:** 5 minutes (add 10 minutes for decorating option)

## Materials Needed

1 inexpensive plain pocket folder per child
1 piece of notebook paper per child
1 wrapped prize per child
1 red marking pen

## Preparation

Before the party - mark all of the papers with an "A" and another symbol such as a plus, a happy face, a star, a heart, etc. For example: A+, A☺, A★, A♥. Slip one sheet of paper into the inside pocket of each folder. Wrap and label gifts with matching symbols to correspond to each "A" paper.

Before you play - seat the children in a circle.

## Introducing the Game

"Your papers have been graded, let's see if you've all passed the party test!"

## How to Play

Mix up the folders and hand them out to the children in random order. Announce to the children they can open their folders to reveal their grade for the party. Turn in your test paper for a corresponding prize.

## Decorating Option

Tuck a sheet of stickers into the pocket of each folder. Supply color marking pens to decorate and personalize the folders as an added activity. This decorating option will add 10 minutes to your game time.

**Prizes:** School supplies and coloring books.

**Favors:** Everyone keeps their folder for "making the grade."

# PICNIC ON AN ANT HILL

**For Ages:** 4 to 10

**Time:** 3 minutes

**Materials Needed**

1 dinner or luncheon napkin per child
1 large box of raisins
2 to 3 yards of ribbon

## Preparation

Before the party - open one napkin and place 10 raisins in the center. Gather the ends and tie with a ribbon. Make one for each child and prepare one napkin with 15 raisins for the winner.

Before you play - seat the children in a circle. Hand out one "picnic blanket" napkin to each child.

## Introducing the Game

"It seems our picnic is being invaded. We need to find who's stirring up the army of ants."

## How to Play

Have the children open the napkins and count the "ants" (raisins). The child with 15 "ants" is picnicking on top of an ant hill and started the invasion. Announce "quick, everybody eat the 'ants' before they ruin the picnic."

**Prizes:** "Chocolate covered ants!" (chocolate covered raisins).

**Favors:** Raisins for everyone.

# QUICK DRAW 101

**For Ages:** 8 to 12

**Time:** 8 minutes

## Materials Needed

1 chair or stool
1 piece of paper per child
1 pencil per child
1 kitchen timer
a hard surface for the children to draw on
  such as a table or 1 book or magazine each

## Preparation

Before the party - none.

Before you play - seat the children at a table or in a circle (use the books or magazines as drawing boards). Set the chair in the middle of the room and hand out the paper and pencils.

## Introducing the Game

"Welcome to your first day of art class 'Quick Draw 101.' The model for our class today will be the guest of honor."

Seat the guest of honor in the model's chair after you introduce the game.

## How to Play

The assignment for this speed drawing course is to draw a picture of the "model" on your piece of paper in only 3 minutes. Use the kitchen timer to assist you in keeping time.

Declare all of the portraits a work of art as they represent how each guest sees their friend. Create an art gallery by taping the signed drawings onto the wall or place on the refrigerator with magnets. Give the children an opportunity to view all of the sketches. Let the "model" keep the drawings to put in a scrapbook as a remembrance.

**Prizes:** Because the children have "sold" their artwork to the guest of honor, award paper money as a prize to everyone.

# STICKS AND STONES

**For Ages:** 4 to 12

**Time:** 6 minutes

## Materials Needed

1 large plastic bowl
1 package of pretzel sticks
   per 8 children
1 lb. of "M & M's®" Peanut
   Chocolate Candies
   per 8 children
1 resealable sandwich bag
   per child

## Preparation

Before the party - fill the bowl with "sticks and stones" (pretzel sticks and "M & M's®" Peanut Chocolate Candies).

Before you play - have the children wash their hands or give them moist towelettes to clean up. Seat the children in a circle around the bowl. Hand out one sandwich bag to each child.

## Introducing the Game

"Sticks and stones may break your bones, but pretzels and candy will never harm you!"

## How to Play

Each child will take a turn to grab one handful from the bowl and place it immediately in the sandwich bag and seal. After everyone has taken one handful, have them count their "M & M's®" Peanut Chocolate Candies to see who collected the most "stones."

**Prizes:** The winner can grab one more handful from the bowl.

**Favors:** Everyone keeps their bag of "sticks and stones" (pretzel sticks and "M & M's®" Peanut Chocolate Candies).

# STORYBOOK MEMORY GAME

**For Ages:** 3 to 10

**Time:** 3½ minutes per illustration

## Materials Needed

1 picture storybook

## Preparation

Before the party - select a picture storybook with detailed illustrations on several open pages.

Before you play - seat the children in a circle.

## Introducing the Game

"We will be mind reading this story to see if you have picture perfect, photographic memories."

## How to Play

Turn to the first fully illustrated page and hold up the book for about 15 to 20 seconds so all of the children can get a good look at the picture. You may need to circle the group of children so all may see the picture clearly. Turn the book towards you and ask some simple questions about the picture. Who is the main character? What kind of shoes was he or she wearing? Was he or she wearing a hat? Was there a car or a bicycle in the picture? Were there any animals, what kind? Add silly questions: Was the birthday child in the picture? Was there a whale driving the bus? The sillier, the better. Alternate silly and serious questions.

Let the children work together for the answers and tell them if they've answered correctly. See how much they can remember from the page in the storybook. Announce they all have picture perfect memories.

Turn to another fully illustrated page with a different scene if they'd like to play again. Ask 6 to 8 questions per picture.

**Favors:** Bookmarks.

# WINNING STATS

**For Ages:** 6 to 12

**Time:** 2 minutes
per winning stat

**Materials Needed**

1 baseball card per child
(same brand) and extra
cards for the winners

**Preparation**

Before the party - separate the cards by pitcher and player. Make sure you have at least one pitcher or one player card per child.

Before you play - shuffle and deal one player <u>or</u> pitcher card to each child.

## Introducing the Game

"Check your baseball player's statistics to see if he's a winner."

## How to Play

Choose a category and announce it to the children, for example: For pitchers, "who has the most games won for the current year?" (check how the statistics are listed on the cards, by past or current years). Award the winning card holder choice of another trading card from those not dealt. Announce another pitching statistic and ask for the highest achiever. Continue until you run out of extra playing cards for prizes.

If player cards are dealt, ask for the most R.B.I.'s, home runs or highest batting average.

**Prizes:** Baseball cards.

**Favors:** Everyone keeps their game playing card.

# Active Games

Alternating active and quiet games is a very good idea for any occasion. These exciting and lively games were designed to complete a well-balanced schedule of activities. See the samples on pages 6 and 7 to see how active games are used to balance a party game plan.

# BOWLING ALLEY CATS

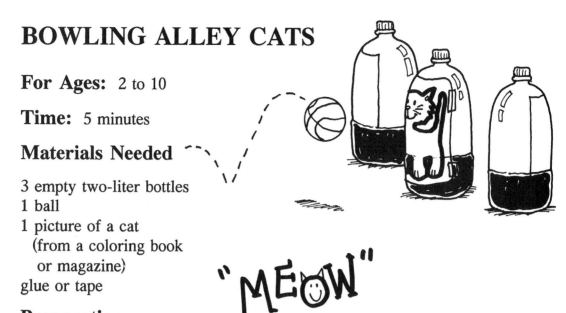

**For Ages:** 2 to 10

**Time:** 5 minutes

**Materials Needed**

3 empty two-liter bottles
1 ball
1 picture of a cat
  (from a coloring book
   or magazine)
glue or tape

## Preparation

Before the party - adhere a picture of a cat to one of the 3 two-liter bottles.

Before you play - set up the pins with the cat as the head pin. Make sure the picture of the cat is facing the children.

## Introducing the Game

"The alley cat has been howling outside your window all night. Roll the ball to him to see if he wants to play."

## How to Play

Each child will be allowed 2 attempts to knock down the pin with the alley cat's picture. The other children need to pay close attention because as soon as the alley cat is knocked down they have to sound off with a loud "MEOW." This will keep them interested in the game until it's their turn to bowl.

**Prizes:** The fun of meowing is the reward.

**Favors:** See if your local bowling center will give you discount or free game coupons for the children at your party or special event. Some bowling centers will enjoy the free promotion.

# CHARCOAL GRAB

**For Ages:** 4 to 12

**Time:** 10 minutes

**Materials Needed**

1 large barbecue or oven mitt
1 roasting pan
40 empty black 35mm film canisters
　　(Ask your friends and family to
　　save theirs. A local film developer
　　may be willing to donate all you
　　need from their recycling bin.)
1 piece of paper
1 pencil

## Preparation

Before the party - fill the roasting pan with the "charcoal" (film canisters). Make a list of the children's names.

Before you play - none.

## Introducing the Game

"It's time to clean out the barbecue pit as fast as you can, but use the barbecue mitt so you won't burn your hand."

## How to Play

Each child will have a turn to grab as many "charcoal briquettes" as possible in 15 seconds with an oven mitt on their hand. No scooping allowed! Count and record the number of "coals" grabbed by each child. Award the child with the most "coals" grabbed a prize. Be prepared for tie winners. Host a "charcoal" grab-off or award prizes to all tie winners.

**Prizes:** Homemade sock puppets.

**Favors:** Fill the film canister "coals" with penny candies or small prizes and distribute equally among the children.

# IN FOR A LANDING

**For Ages:** 2 to 12

**Time:** 5 minutes

## Materials Needed

1 balsa wood flier or 1 piece of paper per child
1 picnic table or 1 large piece of posterboard
1 marking pen

## Preparation

Before the party - if you do not have a picnic table or surface to designate as the "runway," draw a runway on a large posterboard as the target for the airplanes to land on.

Before you play - allow the children to fold their own paper airplane, you may need to help the younger ones.

## Introducing the Game

"Pilot your plane to a safe landing on the runway."

## How to Play

The children will take turns bringing their planes in for a safe landing on the designated "runway."

**Favors:** Everyone keeps the balsa wood flier or the paper airplane as a favor.

# MUTINY IN THE BOTTLE

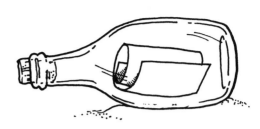

**For Ages:** 5 to 12

**Time:** 10 minutes

## Materials Needed

1 wading pool, water
1 mop
1 white sheet
1 piece of cardboard or sidewalk chalk for a plank
4 empty, clear plastic juice or water bottles
4 rubber bands
4 pieces of paper
1 pencil

## Preparation

Before the party - write each of the following mutiny consequences on a separate piece of paper:

*"Walk the Plank"*        *"Fold the Main Sail"*

*"Swim With the Sharks"*        *"Swab the Deck"*

Roll up each piece of paper and bind with a rubber band. Put one mutiny message in each bottle and secure the cap.

Before you play - set up the cardboard plank or draw one on the sidewalk with chalk. Fill the wading pool with water and send the bottles out to sea. Stir the water to mix up the messages.

## Introducing the Game

"The mutiny you've committed is perfectly clear, you're having too much fun and the price you'll pay is dear."

## How to Play

Select the first group of 4 children to choose one bottle each. Each of the children will take a turn to open their bottle and act out their mutiny orders accordingly:

*"Walk the Plank"* - Walk heel to toe within the plank without falling off.

*"Swim With the Sharks"* - Walk three large circles inside the wading pool.

*"Fold The Main Sail"* - Fold the white sheet neatly and as fast as you can.

*"Swab the Deck"* - Swab everyone's bare feet with a wet mop.

Roll up, rubber-band the notes and send them out to sea in the bottles once again. Choose the next group of 4 children to select a bottle and have their fun at acting out their mutiny consequences. Continue until everyone has a turn at being a pirate.

**\*Safety Tip:** Make sure the mop is clean and free of debris. Supervise their swabbing and collect the mop immediately after the chore is done.

**Favors:** Gold chocolate coins or eye patches made from black felt squares and elastic string.

# SHAKE, RATTLE AND ROLL

**For Ages:** 2 to 12

**Time:** 2 minutes per round

## Materials Needed

1 pair of large fuzzy or satin dice (If you can't find a pair, make your own with two fold-up square gift boxes. Draw dots for die counts with a marking pen on each box. Fill the boxes with equal amounts of tissue or crumpled newspaper for better rolling results.)

## Preparation

Before the party - wrap several prizes for the winning rollers.

Before you play - none.

## Introducing the Game

"Shake, Rattle and Roll for doubles."

## How to Play

Each child will take a turn rolling the dice. If they roll "doubles" (two of the same count), they immediately select a wrapped gift. If you have prizes left, you may want to play another round or continue to roll until all of the prizes have been won. Make sure everyone has an equal amount of rolls, if you run out of prizes, hand out treats.

**Prizes:** Miniature playing cards, jacks, play putty and yoyos.

# SNAKE CHARMING

**For Ages:** 4 to 12

**Time:** 3 minutes
per round

**Materials Needed**

1 three-to-five foot
toy rubber snake
(If you don't have
a toy rubber snake,
use a belt with a
buckle as the snake's
head and a little
imagination.)

## Preparation

Before the party - none.

Before you play - seat the children in a circle.

## Introducing the Game

"Charming a snake, how is it done? Hand over hand and one by one."

## How to Play

The host or party helper will stand in the middle of the circle and hold the snake up by the head. The birthday child will begin the game by grabbing the very tail of the snake. Keep hand in place as the next child (proceed clockwise or counter clockwise) places his hand directly above the first child's grasp. Move the snake around the circle (the children will release their grip as you continue hand over hand) until the head of the snake rests completely within the palm of a child's hand. The winner is the child whose hand completely covers the head of the snake. This fast moving game can be played again and again. Start with another child and move in the opposite direction for a new winner.

**Prizes:** Small rubber snakes.

**Favors:** Give all snake charmers a favor for charming the snake; gummy worms or flute whistles.

# A STONE'S THROW

**For Ages:** 4 to 10

**Time:** 10 minutes

## Materials Needed

1 paper lunch sack
  per child
1 marking pen
newspaper
packaging tape
crayons

## Preparation

Before the party - personalize each lunch sack with the name of a guest. Stuff the bags with crumpled newspaper and seal with packaging tape to resemble stones.

Before you play - have the children decorate their "stones" with crayons.

## Introducing the Game

"This party is a stone's throw away from the giant rock quarry on the other side of the hill (yard, fence, house, etc.). Toss the stones back into the quarry."

## How to Play

Each child will throw their "stone" as far as they can from a designated line. Determine the winner by picking up the stone that was thrown the farthest and announce the name on the "stone."

**Prizes:** A bag of candy "pebbles", "M & M's®" Peanut Chocolate Candies.

**Favors:** Everyone keeps their decorated "stone."

# TABLETOP SHUFFLEBOARD

**For Ages:** 4 to 12

**Time:** 5 minutes

## Materials Needed

1 picnic or card table
1 metal jar lid (from mayonnaise, pickles or baby food)
1 spatula
1 removable label per child or a roll of masking tape
1 ink or marking pen

## Preparation

Before the party - write one child's name on each of the removable labels or on pieces of masking tape.

Before you play - clear the table.

## Introducing the Game

"Practice your shuffleboard skills for the next time you board a cruise ship."

## How to Play

Each child will take a turn using the spatula to send the jar lid from one end of the table to the other. The goal is to get as close to the opposite edge of the table without going over. Mark where the jar lid stops with the personalized label or piece of masking tape after each child's turn. If the lid flies off the table, you won't need to mark the spot. After everyone has taken one turn, look for the winning label or piece of masking tape. It will be the name closest to the opposite edge of the table.

**Prizes:** Award the winner the "game lid" and a special prize.

**Favors:** Throw confetti for a "bon voyage."

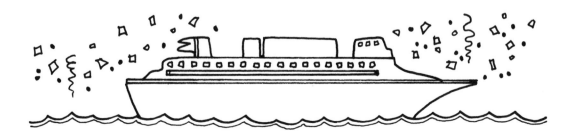

# WOODEN SPOON GOLF

**For Ages:** 2 to 12

**Time:** 7 minutes

## Materials Needed

1 long handle wooden spoon
1 ping pong ball
1 empty frozen juice can

## Preparation

Before the party - rinse the juice can and let dry.

Before you play - none.

## Introducing the Game

"Concentrate on putting a hole-in-one in the juice can."

## How to Play

Each child will have 3 attempts to putt the ping pong ball into the juice can. Gauge the distance by the abilities of your guests (let your children practice before the party to see how well they do). Give the little ones a handicap by allowing them to line up their ball closer to the can.

## Game Tip for Toddlers

Toddlers will really enjoy this game if you can equip each of them with a complete golf set; an empty paper towel roll for a putter, a ping pong ball and an empty juice can. They can putt all 18 holes. Allow each toddler to keep their golf set as a favor.

**Prizes:** Hole-in-one flag pencils; hot glue a small felt triangle to the top of an unsharpened pencil, just below the eraser. This prize is not recommended for children under 5 years of age.

**Favors:** Serve donut holes (in-one) for a snack.

# Ready-to-Copy Games

"Ready-to-Copy" games are ideal for any occasion. All you have to do is make the copies before the party and hand them out with pencils and crayons at game time. These games are noncompetitive, so the children may enjoy a paper challenge at their own pace. When their project is complete, they can color the picture.

If you choose a "Ready-to-Copy" game for your schedule, plan on approximately 10 minutes. The time will vary according to the ages and abilities of the children. The games in this chapter would make great extra games and farewell activities.

# CAKE DECORATING
Add features and "frost" with crayons.

# FUNCASTLE MAZE
Help the frog find the castle
filled with fun.

# MAD HATTERS

Unscramble the words
to identify the hats
in the stack.

\_ \_ \_ \_ \_ \_

L R I S O A

\_ \_ \_ \_ \_ \_ \_ \_

M E O S B R R O

\_ \_ \_ \_ \_ \_ \_ \_

A B L S E A L B

\_ \_ \_ \_ \_ \_

E R P T A I

\_ \_ \_ \_   \_ \_ \_ \_ \_

R E F I        H F C E I

\_ \_ \_ \_

E C F H

\_ \_ \_ \_ \_ \_

Y O O B W C

\_ \_ \_   \_ \_ \_

P T O        A H T

(solution on page 120)

# STAR GAZING

Match the stars in the sky to the stars in the sea.
If each had a twin, which one would it be?

# TREEHOUSE CUT, PASTE AND COLOR

Decorate your treehouse with these designer cut-outs,
add some decor of your own and color.

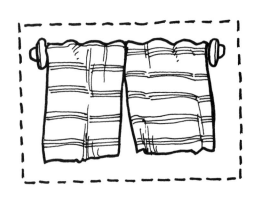

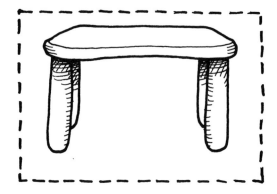

# UNDER MY BED

Circle the things you would find under your bed, put an X on the things you wouldn't (or shouldn't) find under your bed and color.

(solution on page 121)

# WORD SEARCH FUN

```
P  U  N  C  H  D  B  L  T  N  E  X  K  A  J  S  D
I  S  X  G  L  B  E  A  W  B  L  C  P  I  K  T  F
C  V  D  X  P  A  Y  O  D  I  R  F  R  S  Q  M  R
E  B  H  Z  E  L  T  K  A  R  O  G  A  T  Z  N  I
C  A  K  E  J  L  E  M  Y  T  C  A  L  V  B  H  E
R  F  P  N  Q  O  R  U  A  H  P  M  W  C  O  Z  N
E  B  G  I  W  O  V  K  T  D  X  E  Z  A  L  R  D
A  U  D  L  O  N  F  R  Q  A  J  S  I  G  P  W  S
M  Z  N  K  D  S  E  O  R  Y  T  A  M  C  L  D  J
B  I  H  V  X  G  I  F  T  S  F  R  O  E  Z  A  K
```

Find these words and circle for birthday party fun!

| | |
|---|---|
| **BALLOONS** | **GAMES** |
| **BIRTHDAY** | **GIFTS** |
| **CAKE** | **ICE CREAM** |
| **FAVORS** | **PUNCH** |
| **FRIENDS** | |

(solution on page 120)

*permission to photocopy by Funcastle Publications*™

# ZOO "FINDERS" KEEPERS

Help the zoo keeper find these things hiding at the zoo.

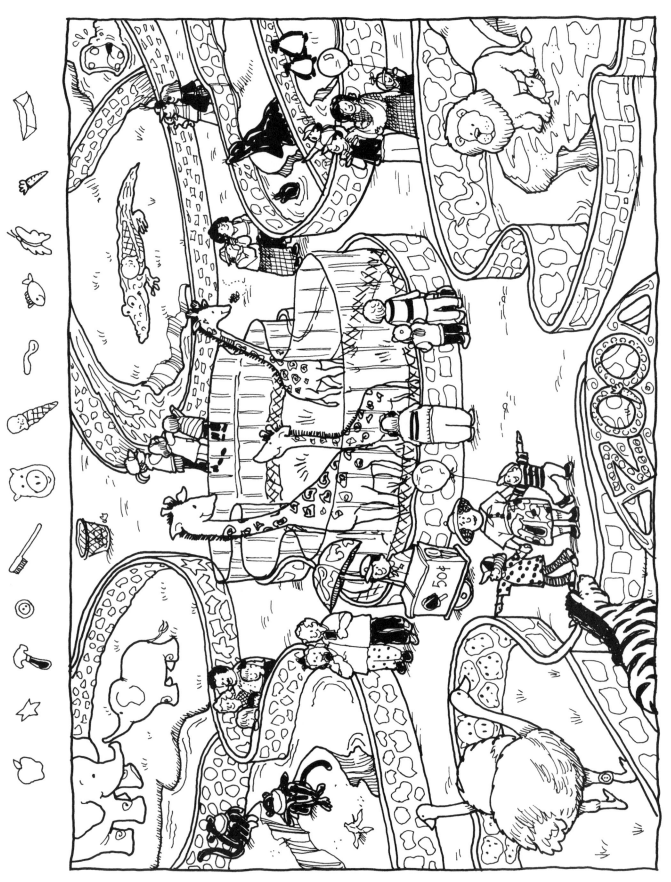

(solution on page 121)

# Noncompetitive Activities

Some children may not be familiar with the concept of a noncompetitive activity, so before you play these games be sure to announce they're "just for fun." You'll see them breathe a sigh of relief and relax as you begin to explain the rules of the game.

Although it's typically younger children (under 8 years of age) who are sensitive to defeat or haven't quite developed good sportsman-like behavior, these activities are great for any age. Children deserve a break from competition, just as much as we do. It's nice not having to be on your toes all of the time.

# CATCH OF THE DAY

**For Ages:** 2 to 10

**Time:** 5 minutes

## Materials Needed

1 mesh laundry bag or pillow case
1 empty laundry hamper or toy box
1 wrapped prize per child

## Preparation

Before the party - empty the laundry hamper or toy box.

Before you play - seat the children in a circle.

## Introducing the Game

Describe how a fisherman will cast his net into the sea from the side of his boat, hoping to catch a bounty of fish. He waits until the end of the day to reel in his "catch of the day." As the birthday child lowers the net into the "sea" (laundry hamper or toy box), ask the children what they think the net will bring. Add some humor by announcing you may catch a tire, an old shoe, a crabby crab or anything else they may find humorous. Let the children know that everyone will be able to see the "catch of the day" toward the end of the party.

## How to Play

After the net has been dropped into the "sea," lead the children in the remaining games and activities planned for the party.

Later, while your guests are busy eating cake and ice cream, secretly place the wrapped prizes in the net and return it to the "sea" (laundry hamper or toy box). When the refreshments are cleared away, invite the children to gather around the "sea" (laundry hamper or toy box). The birthday child will retrieve the net and discover a bountiful catch. Spill the contents onto the "deck" and allow each child to select a "catch of the day."

## Special Touch

Add an old shoe, a tire from a toy truck or tricycle, a toy crab or all of the above. Add sea shells, toy sea creatures and gold doubloons (chocolate coins).

**Prizes:** Plastic float animals, small toy boats, fun shape bath soaps and gifts from the sea.

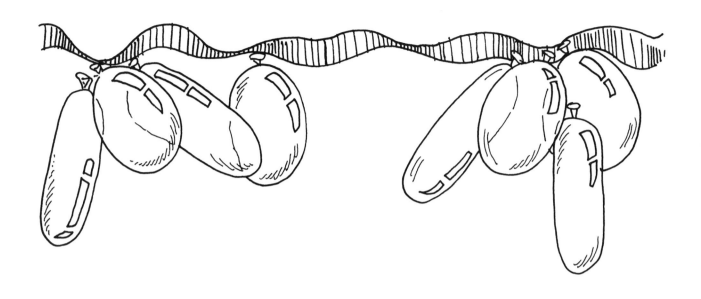

# CREEPY CRITTERS

**For Ages:** 8 to 12

**Time:** 10 minutes

## Materials Needed

This game is for an overnighter, so you will need:

1 sleeping bag per child
1 plastic toy spider or snake

## Preparation

Before the party - none.

Before you play - make sure the sleeping bags are unrolled and ready to crawl into for the night. Seat the children in a circle away from the sleeping area.

## Introducing the Game

"With a little help from your friends, creepy critters might be hiding in your bed?"

## How to Play

The children will cover their eyes while the birthday child hides the "creepy critter" (toy spider or snake) in one of the children's sleeping bags. When the birthday child returns to the circle, the children will run and check their own sleeping bag for the "creepy critter." Return to the circle after checking. The child that found the "creepy critter" will hide it next. Play a few more times until the children get tired of running and checking. It's fun finding "creepy critters" in your sleeping bag when you know they won't bite.

**Favors:** A toy spider or snake for each child.

# GIVE THAT DOG A BATH!

**For Ages:** 2 to 10

**Time:** 8 minutes

## Materials Needed

1 large brown paper grocery bag
1 black marking pen
scissors (for preparation only)
1 spray bottle (a plant mister filled with water)
durable tape

## Preparation

Before the party - cut the paper bag along one side, then trim off the bottom and lay flat for a large piece of brown paper. Draw an outline of a dog with the black marking pen. Cut out the dog and decorate with features and a collar. Tape the dog cut-out to a fence or wall.

Before you play - have the children form a single file line.

## Introducing the Game

"Your pet dog refuses to take a bath. It's time to get the garden hose and take aim."

## How to Play

Each child will have a turn to take aim at the "dog" (cut-out) with the "garden hose" (spray bottle). Squirt the "dog" once and move to the end of the line. See how many players it takes to completely soak the "dog" for its bath. If it takes more than one try per child, go through the line again. Let each child have the same amount of turns.

**Favors:** A bottle of bubbles or fun soap for each child.

# HIKING TRAIL SCAVENGER HUNT

**For Ages:** 6 to 12

**Time:** 15 minutes

## Materials Needed

10 items beginning with different
  letters of the alphabet
1 piece of paper
1 pencil

## Preparation

Before the party - list the 10 items alphabetically on a piece of paper. Number the items 1 through 10. The children will work together on one list. Make copies of the list if you have several guests.

Before you play - have the children leave the area while you hide the items, slightly in view, in a zig-zag pattern throughout the yard. Hide item #1 far away from #2 and so on.

## Introducing the Game

"Blaze a new hiking trail by searching for the items on your scavenger list in A,B,C order."

## How to Play

The scavenger hunt begins by searching for item #1 on the list. If another item is discovered, it cannot be picked up until the items listed before it are found. The children must collect the items in alphabetical order. This will encourage everyone to work together (remembering where they spotted item #5 while they were searching for item #1). The children will blaze their own hiking trail by hunting back and forth for items in the order in which they appear on the list.

**Favors:** Make your own trail mix with "M & M's®" Plain Chocolate Candies, raisins, pretzels, banana chips, dry cereal and bite-size crackers. Serve in resealable sandwich bags.

1. Animal Crackers (small box)
2. Apple
3. Ball
4. Dog Collar
5. Gift
6. Macaroni and Cheese (box)
7. Paper Plate
8. Sand Shovel
9. Soap Dish
10. Water Bottle

# LION TAMER

**For Ages:** 4 to 6

**Time:** 5 minutes

## Materials Needed

1 large posterboard
1 large cardboard box
1 wrapped prize
  per child
color marking pens
scissors (for preparation only)
durable tape

## Preparation

Before the party - draw and color a "roaring" lion's face and mane to cover the entire area of the posterboard. The mouth should be open wide enough so that when cut away, a child's head may pass through the opening (round off the points on the teeth so they won't be too sharp). Trace the outline of the lion's mouth only and cut away from one side of the box (it is not necessary to trace and cut the teeth again). Match the openings of the posterboard lion's face with the opening on the box and adhere with tape. Place the prizes in the bottom of the box and secure the lid.

Before you play - have the children form a single file line.

## Introducing the Game

"Who's turn was it to feed the lion? He's eaten all of our prizes because we forgot to feed him. Tame the lion long enough to reach in and grab a prize."

## How to Play

One at a time, each child will "tame the lion" by sticking his head into the lion's mouth. After the child has accomplished this, they may reach into the lion's mouth with one hand and collect a prize from the bottom of the box. Continue until every child has "tamed the lion."

## Game Tip

If a child is hesitant, by all means, "tame the lion" for them. Ask if they'd like to hold your hand while you make the brave attempt to retrieve their prize. If they agree to hold your hand, say "I couldn't have done it without you" as you hand them their prize.

**Prizes:** Gifts with a circus or lion theme: animal cookies, candy circus peanuts, animal toys and books.

# THE MAGIC LAMP

**For Ages:** 4 to 12

**Time:** 10 minutes

## Materials Needed

1 hot/cold paper cup
  with handle
1 "treasure" prize
  per child

## Preparation

Before the party - place one treasure in each cup. Start at the handle and fold down the top of the cup at an angle to resemble a magic lamp. Crease the cup at the fold to secure.

Before you play - seat the children in a circle. Hand out one "magic lamp" to each child.

## Introducing the Game

"The genie in this lamp would like to hear your three wishes. If they are indeed three very good wishes, he will bestow upon you a great treasure."

## How to Play

One at a time the children will rub their lamp and make three wishes for everyone to hear. Offer these suggestions if they seem a little stumped: "I wish I had a puppy," "I wish I didn't have to do my homework," "I wish it were MY birthday." After they've shared their wishes with the other children they may open their lamp for a treasure.

**Game Tip:** For large groups or young children make only one wish.

**Prizes:** Polished stones, chocolate coins, rings, necklaces and craft jewels.

**Favors:** The magic lamp to hold your treasure.

# MAN IN THE MOON

**For Ages:** 4 to 12

**Time:** 10 minutes

## Materials Needed

yellow construction paper
  (1 piece per 4 children)
scissors
  (for preparation only)
1 pencil
several black marking pens
  for the children to share
1 flashlight

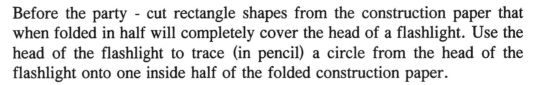

## Preparation

Before the party - cut rectangle shapes from the construction paper that when folded in half will completely cover the head of a flashlight. Use the head of the flashlight to trace (in pencil) a circle from the head of the flashlight onto one inside half of the folded construction paper.

Before you play - none.

## Introducing the Game

"If you could picture the man in the moon, how would he appear on a moonlit night?"

## How to Play

The children use the black marking pens to draw a funny face within the traced circle. Return the paper to its folded position. The host will hold the backside of the drawing directly over the head of the flashlight with the folded flap covering the drawing. The face is hidden and all that is visible is yellow construction paper. Turn on the flashlight to reveal the "man in the moon." Everyone will have a turn to see their hidden picture as the host reveals each "man in the moon" to all of the children.

**Favors:** Everyone can keep their "man in the moon."

# MONKEY SHINES

**For Ages:** 4 to 12

**Time:** 6 minutes

## Materials Needed

1 banana per child

## Preparation

Before the party - none.

Before you play - clear the party area or move to a spot with plenty of room for the children to monkey around.

## Introducing the Game

"It's okay to monkey around in this game where playing with your food is allowed."

## How to Play

The game will begin when you announce the first part of the body that will balance the banana. For example: If you say "inside of your elbow," every one must balance the banana on the inside of their elbow, trying not to drop the banana. There are no eliminations. If you drop the banana you may still continue to play. The next part of the body will be "on your shoulder." Start with the easier feats, then work up to the most difficult, like your nose, head, knee or foot.

**Favors:** Everyone keeps their banana.

# A PIRATE'S REWARD

**For Ages:** 4 to 10

**Time:** 8 minutes

## Materials Needed

1 stuffed toy (or real bird)
 to play the part of the parrot
1 laundry basket (or real cage)
1 plastic shoe box storage container
 or a large plastic bowl
3 lbs. of birdseed
1 pirate's treasure prize per child

## Preparation

Before the party - place the prizes in the container or bowl and add the birdseed.

Before you play - ask the children to name your ship's mascot before you begin. If "Cisco" is a toy parrot, put it inside an overturned laundry basket. If it's a pet bird, move it to the other side of the room.

## Introducing the Game

"The pirates on the other side of the island have rescued your lost mascot, Cisco, the parrot. You wish to reward the pirates for their good deed, but the treasure is hidden away in a chest full of birdseed. Once you uncover the treasure you may pay the pirates and bring Cisco back to your ship."

## How to Play

One at a time, each child will reach one hand into the birdseed to dig for one prize. When everyone has found a treasure, return "Cisco" for all to welcome home.

**Bountiful Treasure Option:** Bury as many treasures as you wish, but make it an even number of prizes per guest. Children like to dig for buried treasure, again and again. Additional rounds will take approximately 6 minutes each.

**Prizes:** Jewelry, chocolate coins, toy fish and assorted small treasures.

## Farewell Activities

Not everyone will be picked up from a celebration at the same time. As the children await their parent's arrival, you can fill the time with crafts or activities that require little or no supervision. This will allow you the freedom to break away and say goodbye to the guests as they leave the party.

# AUTOGRAPH SPORT BALL

**For Ages:** 5 to 12

**Time:** 5 minutes

### Materials Needed

1 large posterboard (white for baseball,
   orange for basketball, brown for football)
scissors (for preparation only)
1 red marking pen (for baseball)
   or 1 black marking pen (for basketball or football)

### Preparation

Before the party - draw an outline of the selected sport ball in pencil and cut from the posterboard. Add the lines or stitched seams with a marking pen.

Before you begin - none.

### How to Make

Each guest can autograph the poster size sport ball as a special remembrance for the birthday child.

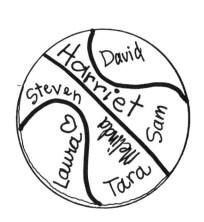

# COURT JESTERS

**For Ages:** 6 to 12

**Time:** 10 minutes

## Materials Needed

1 riddle book (bookstore or library)
1 or more pieces of paper per child
1 pencil

## Preparation

Before the party - write one riddle on each piece of paper and fold. Prepare at least one riddle per child.

Before you begin - none.

## How to Play

The children can take turns sharing a riddle. Some may surprise you with their comedic talents and know quite a few. The prepared riddles will be on hand to assist the children that need help.

# GIFT WRAP ART

**For Ages:** 2 to 12

**Time:** 15 minutes

## Materials Needed

miscellaneous arts and crafts supplies
gift wrap from presents opened at the party
several bottles of non-toxic, white glue
construction paper
children's safety scissors
empty boxes, cartons and containers

## Preparation

Before the party - gather all the miscellaneous arts and craft supplies you can find, including recyclable boxes, cartons and containers.

Before you begin - set up the work table with the art supplies for the children to share. After opening the gifts, save the wrapping paper from the landfill and bring it over to the children's work table.

## How to Make

The children can create gift wrap/recycle art projects.

# MARACAS

**For Ages:** 2 to 4

**Time:** 10 minutes

## Materials Needed

1 plastic fill egg per child
  (save from Easter)
1 package of dry instant white rice
transparent tape
music

## Preparation

Before the party - fill the eggs with one heaping teaspoon of rice, close and seal with tape.

Before you play - hand out one egg "maraca" to each child.

## How to Play

The children can play the "maracas" during a fun-filled music video or sing-along tape.

# PICTURE POSTCARDS

**For Ages:** 2 to 12

**Time:** 10 minutes

## Materials Needed

1  4" x 6" blank index card per child
1 black ink or marking pen
crayons (for toddlers), color pencils or marking pens

## Preparation

Before the party - draw the lines as they appear on the back of a picture postcard on one side of the index card. Prepare one card for each child.

Before you begin - hand out one picture postcard to each child. Supply crayons, color pencils or marking pens for the children to share.

## How to Make

Let the children decorate the "picture" side of the postcard with drawings or colorful designs.

## Special Touch

Give each child a postcard stamp to stick within the small box outlined for postage. Tell them it's ready to drop in the mailbox after they write a short message and fill in the address of a friend or relative.

# PLANT STICKS

**For Ages:** 4 to 12

**Time:** 10 minutes

## Materials Needed

1 ice cream stick (or craft stick)
   per child
1 posterboard
scissors (for preparation only)
hot glue gun
color marking pens

## Preparation

Before the party - draw simple designs on small posterboard cut-outs. Hot glue one cut-out to each ice cream or craft stick. Make one "plant stick" per child.

Before you begin - supply the color marking pens for the children to share.

## How to Make

The children can personalize and color their plant sticks.

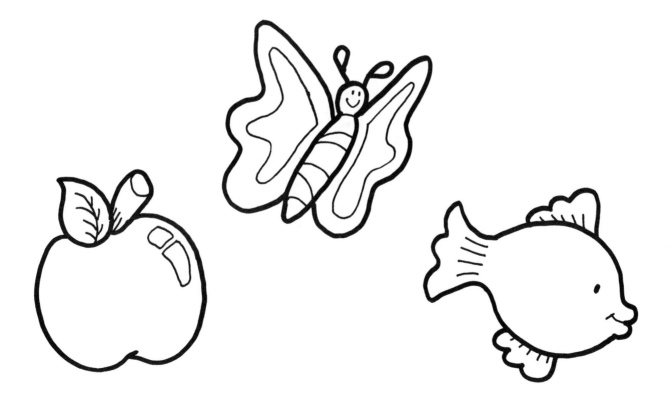

# STAINED GLASS WINDOWS

**For Ages:** 4 to 12

**Time:** 15 minutes

## Materials Needed

1 piece of durable tracing paper per child
1 broad line black marking pen
bright color marking pens

## Preparation

Before the party - draw an outline of a picture on each piece of tracing paper.

Before you begin - supply the color marking pens for the children to share.

## How to Make

The children can color the tracing paper designs with the marking pens. Hold to the light for a beautiful "Stained Glass Window."

# STICK SCULPTURES

**For Ages:** 4 to 12

**Time:** 10 minutes

## Materials Needed

1 economy size package of chenille stems
  6 chenille stems per child would be ideal

## Preparation

Before the party - none.

Before you begin - divide the package equally among the children.

## How to Make

The children can bend, twist and shape the stems to create just about anything. You can even spell your name!

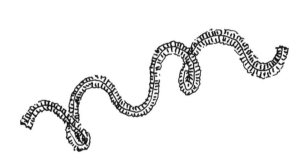

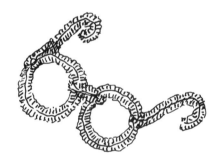

# WISH LIST

**For Ages:** 3 to 12

**Time:** 15 minutes

## Materials Needed

toy catalogs
several children's
  safety scissors
glue sticks
1 piece of construction
  paper per child

## Preparation

Before the party - pick up catalogs at local toy and retail stores or save sale catalogs that come in the mail.

Before you begin - set up the work table with the supplies for the children to share.

## How to Make

The children can cut out pictures of their favorite toys advertised in the catalogs and glue to the paper. They can keep the collages as a head start on their birthday or Christmas wish list.

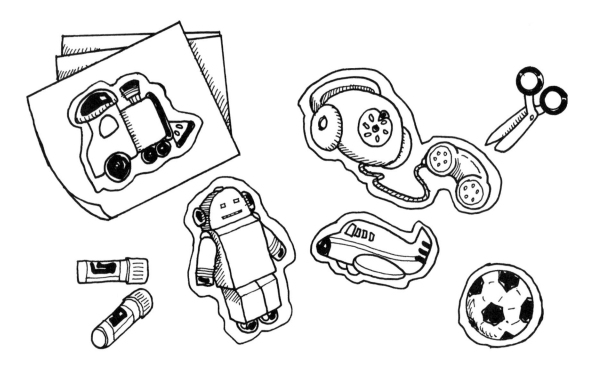

# THEME PARTY INDEX

\*\*\*\*\*\*\*\*\*\*\*\*\*\*\*\*\*\*\*\*\*\*\*\*\*\*\*\*\*\*\*\*\*\*\*\*\*\*\*\*\*\*\*\*\*\*\*\*\*\*\*\*\*\*\*\*\*\*\*\*\*\*\*\*\*\*\*\*\*\*\*\*\*\*\*\*\*\*

# Order Form

*Games Galore for Children's Parties and More* will make a great gift for a friend, relative, teacher, childcare professional or anyone who would appreciate new ideas in entertaining children. Enclose a check or money order in the following amounts as it applies to your residence and quantity of books requested.

In the United States: $9.95 per book + $3.00 shipping for the first book and $1.00 for each additional book (California residents add $.77 sales tax per book)

Canada and overseas: $9.95 per book + $4.00 shipping for the first book and $2.00 for each additional book (checks and money orders must be in U.S. funds)

Send order and payment to: Funcastle Publications, P.O. Box 51217, Riverside, CA 92517     (951) 653-5200

Send *Games Galore for Children's Parties and More* to:

Name: _____

Address: _____City: _____State: _____ Zip:_____

\*\*\*\*\*\*\*\*\*\*\*\*\*\*\*\*\*\*\*\*\*\*\*\*\*\*\*\*\*\*\*\*\*\*\*\*\*\*\*\*\*\*\*\*\*\*\*\*\*\*\*\*\*\*\*\*\*\*\*\*\*\*\*\*\*\*\*\*\*\*\*\*\*\*\*\*\*\*

# READY-TO-COPY GAME SOLUTIONS

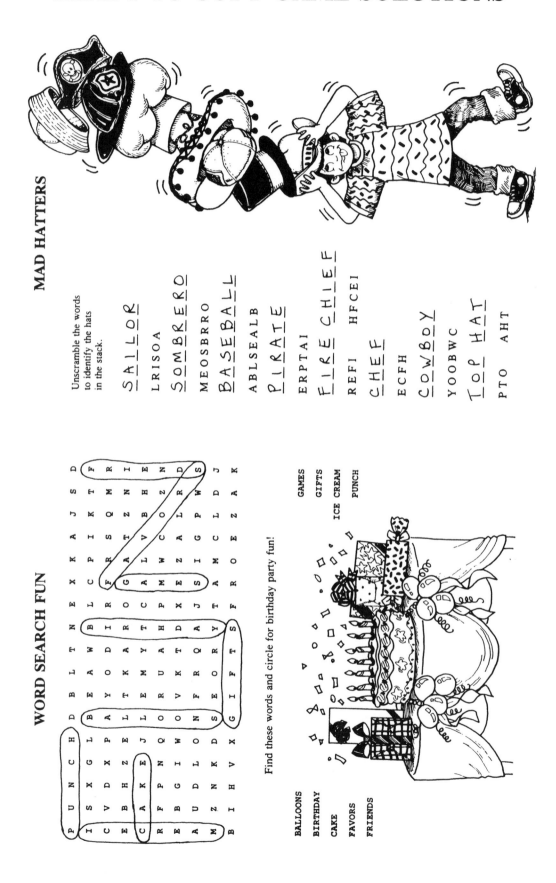

## MAD HATTERS

Unscramble the words to identify the hats in the stack.

LRISOA — S A I L O R

SOMBRERO — S O M B R E R O

MEOSBRRO — S O M B R E R O

ABLSEALB — B A S E B A L L

ERPTAI — P I R A T E

FIRE CHIEF — F I R E C H I E F

REFI HFCEI — 

ECFH — C H E F

YOOBWC — C O W B O Y

PTO AHT — T O P H A T

## WORD SEARCH FUN

Find these words and circle for birthday party fun!

BALLOONS
BIRTHDAY
CAKE
FAVORS
FRIENDS

GAMES
GIFTS
ICE CREAM
PUNCH

# READY-TO-COPY GAME SOLUTIONS

**UNDER MY BED**

Circle the things you would find under your bed, put an X on the things you wouldn't (or shouldn't) find under your bed and color.

**ZOO "FINDERS" KEEPERS**

Help the zoo keeper find these things hiding at the zoo.

May
all of your
celebrations
be
filled with
joy,

Shari

*An Announcement:*

**Our newest addition
will be
arriving in 2006**

**Games Galore
for
Baby Showers**